Peter Cochrane

THE WESTERN FRONT
1916–1918

ABC
Books

Published by ABC Books for the
AUSTRALIAN BROADCASTING CORPORATION
GPO Box 9994 Sydney NSW 2001

Copyright © Peter Cochrane 2004
Photographers copyright © Individual photographers or institutions

First published April 2004

National Library of Australia
Cataloguing-in-Publication entry
Cochrane, Peter, 1950-
The Western Front 1916-1918.
ISBN 0 7333 1280 2.
1. World War, 1914-1918 - Campaigns – Western Front –
Pictorial works. 2. World War, 1914-1918 – Participation,
Australian. I. Australian Broadcasting Corporation. II Title.
940.4272

Cover photographs (front) E01220 and (back) E00833
courtesy of the Australian War Memorial
Designed by Melanie Feddersen, i2i design
Colour reproduction by PageSet, Victoria
Printed and bound in Singapore

5 4 3 2 1

RIGHT: B Company men, 30th Battalion, amongst the ruins of Bapaume on the day the Australians entered the town, 17 March 1917. The documentation of official photographs of the AIF was lost late in the war, so it is not possible to identify who took most official images. In this case, the date suggests Herbert Baldwin, as he was the only official photographer working for the AIF in March 1917. (AWM E00361)

Since the push started everyone has been in wonderful spirits … all are as pleased as punch. The Hun seems to have had all the go knocked out of him.

Captain L. C. Roth, MC, 2nd Pioneer Battalion, 9 April 1917

... a roaring boiling hell of shot and shell and mangled men.

Sergeant A.W. Armstrong, 24th Battalion, AIF, 24 July 1916

CONTENTS

THE WESTERN FRONT

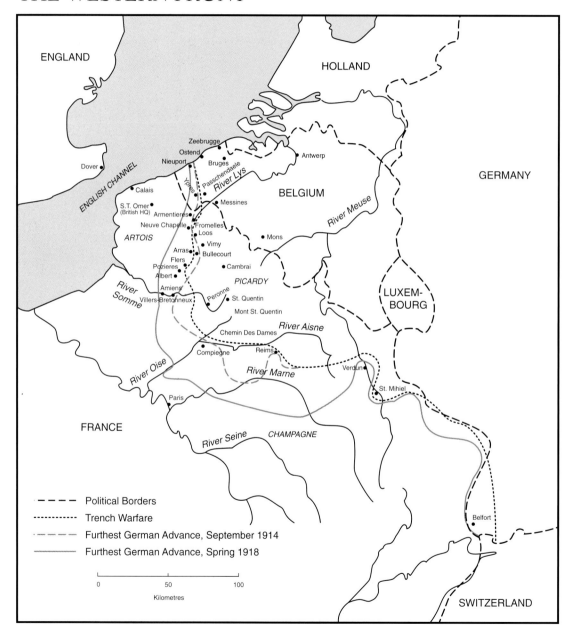

ENGLAND

HOLLAND

GERMANY

ENGLISH CHANNEL

Dover

Zeebrugge
Ostend
Nieuport
Bruges
Antwerp

Calais

S.T. Omer
(British HQ)

Passchendaele

River Lys

BELGIUM

Ypres

Messines

River Meuse

Armentieres

Neuve Chapelle
Fromelles
Loos

ARTOIS

Mons

Vimy

Arras
Bullecourt

Flers

Cambrai

Pozieres
Albert

PICARDY

LUXEM-
BOURG

River
Somme

Amiens
Villers-Bretonneux

Peronne

St. Quentin

Mont St. Quentin

River Aisne

Chemin Des Dames

Reims

Compiegne

River Marne

Verdun

River Oise

St. Mihiel

Paris

FRANCE

River Seine

CHAMPAGNE

Belfort

SWITZERLAND

- – – – Political Borders
- ······ Trench Warfare
- – · – Furthest German Advance, September 1914
- ——— Furthest German Advance, Spring 1918

0   50   100
Kilometres

INTRODUCTION

*Wilkins and I pottered around various ruins ...
to fossil out standpoints from which to take
photographs.*

Captain Frank Hurley, Ypres, 28 September 1917

When the Gallipoli campaign ended in December 1915, the Australian Imperial Force (AIF) was hastily reorganised, expanded from two Divisions to five and readied for action on the Western Front in France. Australian troops landed in Marseilles and journeyed through countryside so green and pretty they could not imagine the war-torn landscapes that awaited them. One of them described the trip across France as 'like a succession of cinematic views of Paradise'. They were merging into the Allied zone near Armentières in northern France from March 1916.

The term 'Western Front' came from the Germans, who distinguished this battle line from their eastern front in Russia. British, French, Canadian, Australian and other troops simply adopted the term as their own. When Australians entered the fray on 5 June, the Western Front had already settled into opposing lines of trenches and fortifications that stretched nearly 800 kilometres from the English Channel near Ostende in Belgium to Belfort on the French–Swiss border. A stalemate had set in. Despite massive blood-letting and slaughter, there was to be no great change in this front for another two years. The scything of machine guns at 500 bullets per minute, and the awesome power of the artillery barrage, favoured defence over attack and compounded an impasse that remained unbroken until the German offensive of March 1918.

Who will return? Men of the 53rd Battalion waiting to don their equipment for the attack on Fromelles, 19 July 1916. Only three of those shown here came out of the action alive and they were wounded. (Donated by L-Cpl. C. H. Lorking, 53rd Battalion. AWM A03042)

Millions of men faced each other across the killing grounds of the Western Front. Their ordeal alternated between tedious weeks of static siege and marathon bouts of earth-shaking, furious battle. In most parts of the line, soldiers were entrenched. They were immured in dugouts and tunnel networks, they lived behind fire steps and sandbagged parapets and thickets of barbed wire bordering a no-man's-land of crater-like shell holes, skeletal trees, shreds of human flesh and shards of discolouring bone. The worst of the battlefields became pulverised ground — earth red with rust and wet with blood, or otherwise churned into sucking mud. Here lay the litter of mad infantry charges: rifles, cartridge shells, watches, packs, boots, bayonets, helmets, false teeth, spectacles, a water bottle, the pathetic ephemera of wrecked pockets; dead and dying, some strung out on the wire, others half buried under breakers of dirt or mud. And sounds — terrible human sounds — that some survivors would remember for the rest of their lives.

On both sides, the front line fighters endured days and sometimes weeks of artillery bombardment — an opening barrage in a major battle might expend one or two million shells. Soldiers followed their own artillery across the heavily scarred earth and, win or lose, both sides took fearful casualties. At Verdun in 1916, the Germans tried to break the French line. Two million men fought for four months at the cost of a million casualties. The British countered with an offensive near the Somme River that cost them 420,000 dead.

Into this war came the Australians — light-hearted, confident, curious, not easily soured. In their first major battle at Fromelles, the 5th Division was near decimated. Almost half its number became casualties — 5,553 men killed or wounded. One Australian, Brigadier-General H. E. 'Pompey' Elliott, met the survivors with tears streaming down his cheeks. Some battalions in the Division almost folded for want of men. Now they knew the truth

— the Western Front was a wasteland of brutality and suffering, valour and death. It was a landscape, and an experience, beyond the imagination of all who were not there.

THE CAMERA IN WAR

Those who were not there wanted to know what it was like. Australians at home had grown used to images of war in the form of sketches and photographs from Gallipoli. The illustrated newspapers reproduced photos sent by pressmen, by the official correspondent to the AIF, Charles Bean, and by the Admiralty's photographer on the peninsula, Lieutenant Ernest Brooks.

A rare moment off his feet. Captain Charles Bean, the Australian official correspondent, watching the Australian advance near Martinpuich, France, 27 February 1917. (AWM E00246)

Soldiers sent their negatives too. A significant number of them took box brownies or Kodak 'Vest Pocket' cameras to Egypt, confirming that soldiering for King and Country had an element of tourism to it. Many of these cameras were going-away presents. In Egypt, the eager cameramen 'snapped' their mates in training, the Pyramids, the bazaars and anything else that seemed 'exotic', (including themselves) and then they cosseted their prized possession into their packs for the next voyage, the beach landing and the fight. Due to the shortage of pressmen and official photographers, it is the soldier–cameramen who made the greatest contribution to the photographic legacy of the Gallipoli campaign. On the Western Front, the situation was to prove very different.

Photography on the Western Front was not as easy, and images of Australians were scarce for a time. The British government banned the press and they banned cameras too. Except for special duties such as survey or reconnaissance, sketching and photography were entirely prohibited. Soldiers faced disciplinary action if caught taking pictures. Security was one factor; the management of information was another. So strict were the regulations on photography that the English army shot a deaf, amateur landscape photographer late in 1914 — they thought he was a spy. The camera had, in effect, become a weapon of war.

The ban on cameras slowly gave way to a need for propaganda photos. By 1916 the British government, headed by H. H. Asquith, was worried about public opinion at home and abroad. The war in which 'we'll all be home by Christmas' had turned into an epic of appalling attrition with no sign of victory. America had still not joined the fight and the British home front was drained, wearied and increasingly restive. The War Office in London now understood the need for 'military publicity', a relatively new concept. So too did the Foreign Office, anxious to bring the United States into the war. Britain must join that other battle — the battle for hearts and minds. Without compromising the strict control of information, written and visual, the solution was to appoint a small number of professionals to act as official correspondents, photographers and cinematographers.

Early in 1916, two English photographers, Lieutenants Ernest Brooks and Warwick Brooke, were given the job of covering the exploits of the British army — more than two million men under arms — for the newspapers. Their awesome assignment was propaganda photos — 'quantity and variety' — to boost morale at home and to foster friends abroad. This hardly satisfied the Australians who felt, rightly, that their deeds were not getting a fair share of exposure. Charles Bean was told that if he wanted a photographer he might have Brooks or Brooke on temporary loan.

BEAN'S PASSION
Throughout 1916 Bean argued for the appointment of an Australian photographer to cover the Australian war effort exclusively. He knew that the Canadians had won their case in January, mainly through the influence of their man in London, the journalist and entrepreneur Max Aitken (later Lord Beaverbrook). A Canadian photographer attached to the Canadian forces was operating on the Western Front from April 1916.

The morning after. Stretcher-bearers with the dead and wounded at Retaliation Farm after the Passchendaele battle, November 1917. (Hurley. AWM E01202A)

Australia had no advocate in London to compare with Aitken. But Australia did have Charles Bean at the front — a lanky, fine-boned, scholarly type, who was constantly trudging the battlefields taking pictures of his own, along with detailed notes on the deeds of the Australians. He would be their great historian.

Bean wanted to organise a comprehensive collection of written and photographic records covering Australia's part in the war. He was possessed by the idea of collecting images (photographs *and* paintings) for the historical record — an archive for posterity. There was something of a spiritual dimension to his crusade, so moved was he by the suffering and the achievements of his Australians. He later referred to photographs of the AIF as 'sacred records — standing for future generations to see forever the plain, simple truth'. The press wanted the disposable publicity shot — Bean wanted the everlasting image. The press wanted upbeat pictures — Bean wanted authenticity, what he called 'photographs of record'.

The British photographers disappointed him. Their shots were too often fabricated, meaning the composition was pre-arranged, incidents were re-enacted for the camera —

the actors sometimes paid a tot of rum or a pack of cigarettes for their trouble — and even then the negative might be 'doctored' in the darkroom. The morale-boosting purpose of 'news photography' also narrowed the subject matter. News photography emphasised resolve in the trenches, the anticipation of battle, varieties of cheerfulness, the abundance of armaments and munitions, the high spirits of the fighters, the resignation (even happiness) of German prisoners and so on.

Publicity photographs for newspapers often carried a 'Boys' Own' flavour. This one appeared in the *Sydney Mail* (4 October 1916) with a caption that celebrated trophy collecting and the 'adventure' of war.

But soon enough the British photographers, and the War Office in London, came round to the idea of 'record photography'. Both cameramen and politicians acquired a greater appreciation of the historical moment and the need to preserve it in various forms. They also began to see that 'authenticity' was more effective as propaganda. They acknowledged a newspaper readership that was increasingly cynical and more perceptive than it was in 1914. Bean got his way.

Under his occasional direction in 1916, Brooks and Brooke took some valuable pictures — the only official record of the Australians at Armentières, Pozières and Mouquet Farm during 1916. In November that year, an English photographer, Herbert Baldwin, was at last attached to the AIF on a full-time basis and quickly proved himself to be recklessly determined to get authentic 'shots' of men at war. 'If he doesn't look out he'll get taken prisoner — he thinks so too, he's a game little bird,' wrote Bean. In May 1917, an Australian War Records Section (AWRS) was approved for AIF Headquarters in London, formally recognising Bean's call for a national archive. And soon after that, when Herbert Baldwin fell ill with dysentery, two Australian photographers were appointed to replace him.

They were already big names in their chosen field. They were Frank Hurley and Hubert Wilkins.

By chance, Hurley and Wilkins were former polar explorers, one in the Antarctic, the other in the Arctic. They were tough and courageous individuals, accustomed to operating in extreme circumstances, but they were very different personalities. Bean's initial intention was to harness Hurley's flamboyance to the job of publicity work and Wilkins' steadiness to photography for the historical record. But, in the urgency of war, the distinction was blurred and Bean's priority for 'scrupulously genuine' photographs of record is apparent

Men of the 6th Brigade, newly arrived from Egypt, c. April 1916. Responding to the British official photographer, they balance their new steel helmets on their rifles and cheer. (AWM EZ0003)

in the work of both men. The scope of their photography was outstanding. They covered:

… not only the chaos and confusion of the battlefield, its death toll and the strain on the combatants, but also the more mundane details of everyday life, such as health inspections, laundry work and food preparation. There was also an unusual number of interior shots showing officer's dugouts, control posts, and medical dressing stations which indicated both men's mastery of primitive flash equipment gained on their Polar expeditions.

(Jane Carmichael, *First World War Photographers*)

Once the British had conceded the importance of record photography, it was then possible to recognise the importance of Hurley and Wilkins, with provision of their own transport, assistance in the field (a 'camera-lumper'), and freedom to move about as they pleased. Soon there was a small team of Australian image-makers, including several painters and the pen and ink specialist, Will Dyson. At the end of 1917, more photographers were

Flanders, Belguim, 14 September 1917. Captain Frank Hurley (right). Australian official photographer, with his apparatus and assistant. (AWM E01995)

appointed — leave was granted for several non-commissioned officers to take photos in the field. This was belated recognition, but the timing at least enabled good coverage of new themes — the Americans now at the front, the Australian Flying Corps making an impact overhead, and a string of spectacular AIF victories in 1918.

In July 1917, Hurley and Wilkins were posted to Belgium for the Third Battle of Ypres, sometimes called Passchendaele, where the horror of warfare was evident in the statistics — 38,093 Australian casualties. In appalling conditions both men took great risks to get the shots they wanted. Soldiers called them the 'mad photographers'. But Hurley was not satisfied. He was frustrated by the limits of the camera and the difficulties of the environment — a single photographic lens and glass plate could never capture the vastness nor the combined elements of this war. Shells would not burst at the right moment. Aeroplanes failed to time their run to Hurley's dramatic requirements. He made composite photographs by combining several negatives to overcome the bad timing of the elements of war. There was disagreement. For Bean, this was distortion of actuality; for Hurley, it was artistry to match the events — 'I am not even allowed to insert clouds', he moaned. But he did — as can be seen in the photograph on page xi.

In November 1917, Hurley was posted to Palestine to cover the Light Horsemen's war against the Turks. He and Bean would never agree on the question of what was 'authentic'. Wilkins stayed on the Western Front and further enhanced his reputation for daredevilry. Will Dyson wrote that Wilkins was 'one of the bravest men that ever lived'. For his courage he was twice decorated, awarded a Military Cross and Bar. He was the only photographer to receive a combat decoration of any kind. He was our principal photographer on the Western Front.

Is that a chicken leg? Photo by Gunner Barnes of 'An artillery driver's humpy near Beaucourt during the Somme offensive.' After the war Gunner Barnes responded to the Australian War Memorial's call for soldier's photographs. Fifty-three of his pictures are now in the AWM collection. (Lent by Gunner Barnes. AWM C00474)

THE SOLDIER–TOURIST

We do not know how many Australian soldiers took a camera to war. The historian Michael McKernan says it was thousands. He is probably right. Some were already hobby photographers, but most were rank amateurs. The term 'six-bob-a-day tourists' was coined and the troops adopted it, often without irony. Patriotic motives did not get in the way of tourist ambitions. Indeed, many of them saw 'touring' as part of the *quid pro quo*. The chance of death or mutilation was there to contemplate. One of the rewards they expected, almost as a right, was the opportunity to do what tourists do — to climb the Pyramids, to tour the English countryside, to see a chateau, or to photo-graph the ruins of the twelfth-century Cloth Hall at Ypres, then perhaps to write a photo caption to properly document this moment in the tour: 'Originally larger than any shop or shop buildings in Sydney, the Cloth Hall has like the rest of Ypres, gone west.'

Small cameras — small enough for a soldier to carry — were for sale just in time for the First World War. They were cheap, reliable and took lightweight roll film, as opposed to

Captain Hubert Wilkins (right), Australian
official photographer, and Will Dyson,
working near Ronssoy in October 1918.
(AWM E03915)

the cumbersome and fragile glass-plate negatives used in larger
cameras. Their manufacturers emphasised simplicity: 'You press
the button, we do the rest,' piped one Kodak advertisement. The
soldier was targeted too — you could load a Kodak camera
'much as you loaded a rifle' according to one of the promotions.
Indeed, the 'Vest Pocket' Kodak was nicknamed the 'soldier's
camera'. There was a curious overlap between the language of
photography and that of war — 'aim, shoot, capture' — and
soldiers' phrasing was similar too: 'Got one of a ruined
chateau,' wrote a certain Corporal Burrell, as if he was out
sniping. Burrell was not too worried about the ban on cameras
at the Western Front, although he did sometimes lapse into code
in his diary: 'met an old woman with a flock of sheep; got a
"P"', he wrote on 4 August 1917, and a good "P" it was. Some
units had followed orders and sent their cameras home. Some
hid them away for occasional use. Others were able to trust in
officers who did not care, and some officers were taking
photographs with their own cameras.

A photograph was a tangible way of taking possession of places that soldiers visited —
a classic tourist thing to do. It was far more personal than a postcard. It was a record of
travel, proof of being there. Along with other diversions, such as having a shave or
writing a letter, it lent a certain civilian normality to the war. Perhaps most importantly,
it linked the soldier to home and family in an intimate way. Whenever possible, the
soldier–photographer smuggled home his rolls of film or his snaps — a visual record of
his tour and his war, a fragment of an imperilled life. And whatever the subject in these
pictures — exotic, quaint, picturesque, funny, architectural, historic — in a sense, all
were autobiographical. All of them were saying 'Here I am', or 'I was there'.

Photography was also a pleasant break from the rounds of military duty. In the rare cases
where a diary accompanies a surviving soldier's photo album, we read of how
photographic routines were woven into the day. Resting after the horrors of Pozières,

Sergeant Donald E. MacDonald of the 17th Battalion wrote a brief account of a quiet day at Messines, near the soon-to-be-famous Hill 60:

9/9/16: Guards relieved by D. Coy 10am. Poor breakfast. Went for a stroll with Jim round ruined city. Got several snaps of Cathedral and clock tower and other ruins. Damage done is shocking … Took 7 pictures in all. Returned to barracks at 11am. Got 7 letters on 8th, lovely one from Kitty, acknowledgement receipt of 75 snaps, English ones and my photos and letters up to 11 June. Expect to move into the trenches tonight.

The indexed 'snaps' that MacDonald sent to Kitty (in Mosman, on Sydney Harbour's north shore) might have been imagined as the final record of a life ended. He was about to go into another battle and his time at Pozières had been terrifying:

24/6/16: … about an hour later awakened with great fear; fierce bombardment on all sides, guns of all sizes and as light as day almost by the flashes of the guns. I was absolutely afraid to move and curled myself up under greatcoat and tried to stop trembling from cold and fear.

Unlike the official photographers, the soldiers with a camera rarely tried to snap such things as bombardments. In battle they were too busy fighting or just surviving. The albums they put together later are mostly a record of sightseeing en route to war or on leave, or of quiet times in the trenches. Having an amateur

France, 1918. The 'Camera Club' of 41st Battalion, 1st AIF. Each soldier is holding a camera, 16 in all. It is the end of the war — cameras appear miraculously from everywhere. The unauthorised photos taken by ordinary soldiers (and some officers too) are a unique and precious part of the pictorial record on the Western Front. (AWM P01861.005)

'Undesirables'. 'A group of 3rd Divisional Signal Company dispatch riders at Foucaucourt, January 1919.

(Lent by Cpl. A. F. Collin. AWM C04827)

cameraman in the unit was probably good for morale. Something of the ordeal was being registered for posterity. All the men could take heart from that. As for the photographer, he was documenting his experience in a special way. His photos were a personal record of travel, war and mateship, far more intimate and candid than official photography could generally manage. They are a unique and precious part of the photographic record on the Western Front.

Take Private D. Jackson of the 20th Battalion, for instance. He took photos of travel and trench life — many of them over-exposed — and later wrote informative captions for each one. One of his pictures shows a soldier checking his mate for lice, while his sub-text reveals how these pictures were a marker for other events, the sequence of happenings, an *aide-mémoire* for documenting his war:

CHATTING: This soldier has just stripped for a 'chat' (lice) in the front line. When things are quiet soldiers indulge in this luxury as often as possible. The sheet behind him is spread out over the fire step and represents his home for 14 days. Three nights after this photo was taken he routed a German raiding party from this point by emptying his revolver into them.

Private Jackson did not keep a diary. His photos with captions were the record of his travels and his war — a view in and of the trenches. His mates also enjoyed the photographic moments. His photo album, like most others, reveals the collective fun of being photographed. It enabled men to briefly escape the war, to lapse into some light-hearted posing, to 'act up', to invest their deadly existence with a skerrick of normality. Photographs were entertainment as well as documentation. When Charles Bean wanted to photograph men of the 29th Battalion, their adjutant warned him to be sneaky: 'We won't tell them,' he advised, 'or we shall have them rolling in the mud or something.'

Sergeant MacDonald's album reveals a similar bonhomie in the presence of the camera. One of his better shots, taken at Bois Grenier in April 1916, is captioned: 'Baker joking with Palmer by threatening him with bayonet in Fire Bay.'

Perhaps the best evidence for the clandestine hobby of the soldier–photographer was at the time of the Armistice: when the war ended, cameras appeared miraculously from everywhere.

WAYS TO REMEMBER

After the war, popular demand for war photographs was undiminished and promoters of photography were quick to capitalise. Kodak sponsored exhibitions of a select body of Hurley's work (128 pictures in all) in London and in Australian capitals. The purists frowned — the composite photos were immensely popular. Hurley continued to insist on their authenticity: 'In order to convey accurate battle impressions,' he wrote in the catalogue, 'I have made several composite pictures, utilizing a number of negatives for the purpose.'

More exhibitions followed. One that drew many viewers was held at Colart's Studios in Melbourne, featuring colour-tinted blow-ups of 'snapshots taken by members of the AIF whilst on active service abroad'. The exhibition brochure claimed the colouring process was 'a secret one, practiced only by ourselves' and the blow-ups were nearly all produced in Melbourne by 'digger artists' associated with the studio. The captions attached to several snaps revealed something of their origin, for example:

132. Bomb explosion: A remarkable photograph, and one which the photographer is not likely to forget, for both he and his camera were hurled some distance by the shock of the explosion …

An action shot was rare and required a happy outcome. The studio was careful to respect the sensitivities of a community in which one in five men who had departed for the war did not come home. In selecting photos, 'horror and heartbreak' were excluded. The pictures aimed only 'to show enough to comfort those who are longing and craving to see the fields their menfolk trod'. War photographs, it seems, could offer solace to the

An unidentified pilot of the 69th Australian Squadron, No. 3 Australian Flying Corps (AFC), about to leave the hangar at Savy on a bombing operation, 22 October 1917. (Hurley. AWM E01177)

grieving. This fact took the most remarkable turn in a small industry that emerged after the war — families with no photo of their lost son in military uniform could now employ a retouch artist to paint the uniform, complete with medals, onto a pre-war photograph of the departed man, or else onto a studio portrait taken en route to war and mailed home.

Archivists were busy too. The AWRS was incorporated into a new institution, the Australian War Museum, later 'Memorial', (AWM), to be based in Melbourne and then Canberra. The Museum was charged with the preservation of three great memorial collections — the written records, the war trophies, and the official photographs of war. But the gaps in the photographic record were considerable due to the late appointment of the official photographers and the limits of what a small number of men might cover in a war of such vast proportions. To fill those gaps, soldiers' photographs were now acknowledged as a legitimate pictorial resource. In the 1920s, the Museum continued an AWRS program begun at the close of the war to acquire copies of privately held prints and negatives. Today, the AWM holds substantially more unofficial than official photos from the First World War — most of them taken by soldiers. There are more than 36,000 in the collection, the majority of these shot in the Middle East and Gallipoli, perhaps 10 per cent covering Australians on the Western Front. It is a priceless record.

The War Memorial also holds about 7,800 lantern slides made from soldier photos and has a small collection of transcripts of lantern slide lectures — the soldier's handwritten or typed narrative to accompany the slide show. The lantern slides of war were especially popular on soldiers' 'smoke nights', but there was a wider audience for them too. Some soldiers went on tour with their slide show.

War photographs were a small but vital substitute for the pilgrimage to the battlefields or the war cemeteries that most families could never afford. Whether out of grieving or simple curiosity, they had tremendous popular appeal. *The Photographic Record of the War*, the twelfth volume of Bean's official history, was first published in 1923. It sold out nine editions before the next war erupted in 1939. Sales reflected the power of the photographic image and the triumph of a new development in publishing — the mass-produced book of photographs. Whatever critics might say about the manipulation of the image, photographs of war provided a quite wonderful sense of access to history, an encounter with the adventure or horror of real events that mattered to so many people. There was something quite magical, it seemed, in their power to hold forever that 'captured' moment.

Time has not curbed our fascination with these images. These days we know more about how they came to be taken, more about the political, military and, ultimately, archival forces that shaped a photographic heritage. But our understanding in no way diminishes the emotional power. The historian Barbara Tuchman described the physical and psychological destruction of war on the Western Front as so massive that 'it lies like a band of scorched earth dividing that time from ours'. We cannot get around that divide. It defies us, like infinity — but our photographic heritage allows us vivid glimpses across it. Produced by official photographers *and* fighting men, preserved and accessible in archives around Australia, that heritage is a national treasure.

Silhouetted against the sky, a photographic tribute to the anonymous heroes of the AIF, Ypres sector, 5 October 1917. These were Support Troops heading for the front line at Broodseinde Ridge.
(Hurley. AWM E00833)

THE FRONT LINE

The prospect of a term in the front line fills me with all sorts of anticipations. What will the actual trenches be like? What is the feeling of one 'under fire' for the first time?

Sergeant J. J. Makin, 21st Battalion, 11 June 1916

The front line experience varied greatly, depending on where you were and what was going on. Trench life in a quiet sector could be pleasant enough, so long as the weather was reasonable, but in a battle zone it was riddled with anxiety and horror. The quiet sectors compared favourably with Gallipoli because stays in the line were short (three to seven days) and they were followed by escape to rest areas, comforts (including hot food) and possibly a little tourism — encounters with French or Belgian culture. Even the route marches, from one part of the line to another, were a travel experience of sorts.

In the battle zones, trench life was hell. Men were unable to wash. They lived cheek by jowl amid the foul smells of stale food, latrine pits, the acrid reek of high explosive fumes, the unmistakable odour of decomposing corpses and the stench of their own unwashed bodies. Enemy attacks were mostly at dawn or dusk when every man was at 'stand-to', ready to fight. In between, the days might be long and tedious, with men off duty choosing to sleep on the trench floor, or else in 'possies' dug out of the trench walls.

After nightfall the trenches came alive with the movement of water and ration parties, rum details, message carriers, reliefs and reinforcements, officer inspections and stretcher-bearers departing with the sick or wounded. When warfare prevented supplies from getting through, soldiers eked out an existence on cold porridge and hard biscuits, a bit of jam if they were lucky and rationed water for tea boiled over a fire made from ammunition boxes.

An enemy bombardment might go on for days, the trench floors littered with dead and wounded, the living pressed hard against the parapets or curled up in their 'possies', half expecting to be buried alive. You could smell the dead, you could hear the moans of the wounded, the cries and the gibbering of men beyond reach.

Allied artillery action was the precursor to engagement. Men by the thousands went over the top and took their chances in the mayhem of the charge; the wash of gunfire, the frenzy of hand-to-hand fighting in enemy trenches, and the perilous scuttle 'home' across the littered waste of no-man's-land. Soon enough, those who survived these battles became resigned to fate, but that did not curb their determination. 'Tomorrow many men must go to their God …' wrote Captain G. D. Mitchell of the 48th Battalion. 'If I die, I die.'

Later in the war the fighting took on new focus. Soldiers left their set positions in the trenches for fast-moving battles across open ground or they fought, street by street, amoung the ruins of villages and towns.

Front line soldiers. 5th Division men on the Montauban Road near
Mametz, December 1916. (Herbert Baldwin. AWM E00019)

Ready. A moment before the battle of Fromelles, 19 July 1916. Men of the 53rd Battalion waiting to go 'over the top'. (Donated by L-Cpl. C. H. Lorking, 53rd Battalion. AWM H16396)

TOP RIGHT: Near Houplines, France, December 1916. A 39th Battalion man prepares his midday meal in a reinforced and sandbagged trench. (AWM E00084)

Saturday. Took over trenches, 1st line left of Hill 60 last night about 10 pm. Conditions much above expectations ... Rations very good. Meat and potatoes and tea (cold) with bread, tinned stew, jam and butter. Night just too beautiful to be stuck in trenches at war.

Sergeant D. E. MacDonald, 17th Battalion, 10 September 1916

Sgt. Donald E. MacDonald's Western Front photographs were mostly a record of life in the trenches with his mates. In this one, his mate is imitating the enemy at close quarters: 'What a man looks like in PH Gas helmet coming at you, Bois Grenier, France, May 1916.' (Sgt. D.E. MacDonald. Mitchell Library PXB226/160)

Sgt. Donald E. MacDonald, 17th Battalion, took some 250 photographs during his tour of Egypt, Gallipoli and the Western Front. His imagined audience was not his nation but his family and his mates in the Battalion: 'Baker joking with Palmer by threatening him with bayonet in Fire Bay. Bois Grenier, France, April 1916.'
(Sgt. D. E. MacDonald. Mitchell Library PXB226/120)

In all this horror there comes, as by a merciful dispensation of nature, a certain insensibility to all fears, quite simple thoughts pass through one's mind: so it is to end here: Here in this dark mildewed hole in the earth ...

Private D. B. Hartford, 51 Battalion, 31 March 1917

Quiet time. An Australian asleep in his 'possie'. He is in the second line of trenches during the fighting for Bullecourt, May 1917. Daytime was the best time to get some sleep as the trenches came alive with activity under the cover of dark. (AWM E00455)

Australians bathing in a shell hole on the Somme after the fighting
for Bullecourt, 12 May 1917. (Herbert Baldwin. AWM E03925)

Exhausted fighters. Men of the 8th Brigade resting on the western outskirts of Bapaume, when the town was entered by the Australian troops on the heels of the retreating Germans, 17 May 1917.
(AWM E00346)

There were dead and wounded everywhere ... I had to sit on top of a dead man as there was no picking and choosing ... I saw a shell lob about twelve yards away and it lifted two men clean up in the air for about six feet and they simply dropped back dead.

Lieutenant L. J. Martin, 1st Machine Gun Battalion, 31 July 1916

German dead near Hannebeek, after its capture in the Battle of Broodseinde, 20 September 1917. The 5th, 6th and 7th Brigades advanced over this area from Westhoek Ridge, which faintly shows in the distance. The white line (across the centre of the photograph) is a tape track, a canvas strip about 5 centimetres wide, indicating the direction the advancing infantry have taken, for the benefit of those following behind. (AWM E00765)

RIGHT: A machine gun position established by the 54th Battalion during the morning of the attack through Péronne, 2 September 1918. The photograph was taken the following day after enemy posts close by had been destroyed. (AWM E03183)

FAR LEFT: *Over the Top*, France 1918. This was the most famous of Frank Hurley's composite photographs. The print that appeared in Hurley's London exhibition (May – September, 1918) was estimated to be 6.5 by 4.5 metres in size and was one of six composite prints in the exhibition. Hurley insisted that his composites allowed him to depict the real drama of battle — a case of the artistry needed to match real events. His superior, Charles Bean, was horrified. Bean believed that Hurley's composite photos were pure distortion. (Hurley. AWM E05988A)

LEFT: Australian troops leaving their trench for an attack somewhere in the Ypres sector. This was one of the photographs that Hurley used for his composite *Over the Top*. (Hurley. AWM E05429)

The tension affected the men in different ways. I couldn't stop urinating, and we were all anxious for the barrage to begin. When it did begin it seemed as if the earth had opened up with a crash. The ground shook and trembled and the concussion made our ears ring.

Lieutenant B. W. Champion, 1st Battalion, 23 July 1916

PHOTOGRAPHERS ON LOAN —

LIEUTENANT BROOKS AND LIEUTENANT BROOKE

The valuable pictures which constitute the only photographic record of the Australians at Armentières, Pozières and Mouquet Farm were thus taken by the British official photographers.

C. E. W. Bean, *The Photographic Record of the War*

Early in 1916, the War Office in London lifted its ban on photographers on the Western Front. This change of policy was in keeping with the now urgent need for propaganda photos. One official photographer was appointed, then another, and then some provision was made for press photographers and even cinematographers to cover the British effort. But no such facilities were extended to the AIF. Throughout 1916, the Australians had to rely on the occasional 'loan' of the two British official photographers, Lieutenant Ernest Brooks and Lieutenant John Warwick Brooke. Brooks was an experienced war photographer having worked for the Admiralty at Gallipoli. Brooke, already in the ranks in France, was the nominee of press proprietors in England.

From mid-1916 they covered the experience of the AIF whenever they could, working in co-operation with Charles Bean. They took morale-boosting photos. Their pictures were published in the illustrated newspapers with cheery captions, such as: 'Here we have some of our victorious gunners with a pile of shells which are to pound the German trenches level with the earth' (*Illustrated London News*, 7 October 1916). The darker side of battle was not entirely overlooked, with some photographs of slightly injured soldiers in the capable hands of ambulance men, but the true grimness — slaughter panoramic — was ignored, judged unfit for publication.

The pictures taken by the two lieutenants of Australian efforts in 1916 are all the more valuable because they are the only official record that we have from that year — a year in which optimism turned to grim endurance. Their photos capture the expectation of battle if not its reality. They document daily routines during quiet times in the trenches, busy times behind the lines, the coming and going of front line fighters and fraternisation with the local people while on leave. There are also some fine action shots, such as 'Limbers at the Gallop, Pozières'.

The case of the photographers on loan is a reminder of the connection between what we see in a photo and the circumstances of its taking. This applies to all photos taken on the Western Front. How the pictorial record of war came to be compiled enables us to understand something of its extent and limits; it allows us to better appreciate the content of the photographs. It enables us to see more.

*Note the French womenfolk
with baskets. Lovely cakes,
fruit, etc., etc. purchasable.*

Sergeant D. E. MacDonald, 17th Battalion, 23 March 1916

Good relations. A warrant officer with the 2nd Australian Pioneer Battalion buys chocolate from a Frenchwoman, some time in 1916. Good relations with local townspeople and farmers was one of the British official photographers' familiar themes. (AWM EZ0108)

Group portrait of 5th and 6th Brigade men, c. June 1916, resting near an ammunition dump during their march to the front line trenches.

(AWM EZ0074)

A carefully composed group portrait of Australian soldiers at the breastworks south-east of Armentières, c. June 1916. Two of the men are 'chatting' (picking lice from their shirts), one reads the newspaper, another looks on with bayonet in hand. (AWM EZ0009)

Sausage Valley near Pozières, 28 August 1916. At this time the valley was a supply line to the front. Beyond the Rolls Royce Phantom are several busy field kitchens. (AWM EZ0113)

Australian gunners at Pozières, 1916. (EZ0147)

Dinner consists of some bully beef and bread and half a slice of margarine and jam. While our water bottles hold out, we can generally make a Dixie of tea.

Private D. Jackson, 20th Battalion, 1916

TOP: Near Pozières, c. June 1916. Having delivered ammunition supplies to the guns, members of an Australian ordnance corps gallop past a dangerous crossroad. (AWM EZ0073)

LEFT: Dashing men. Australian transport limbers gallop past a battery of British 4.7-inch quick-firing field guns, June 1916. The transports are returning from the front at Pozières. (AWM EZ0072)

RIGHT: Infantrymen of the 2nd Australian Division moving away from the front line, c. June 1916. They have a smoke and a chat while posing for the photographer. (AWM EZ0016)

The idea of the never-ending battle. An old French veteran of the 1870 Franco-Prussian war shakes hands with two Australian soldiers in a French village. Other villagers look on. (AWM EZ0034)

A great publicity shot. Group portrait of Australian soldiers sporting helmets (*Pickelhauben*) and caps captured from the Germans in the battle of Pozières. Some have their hands raised for the camera in a feigned gesture of surrender. (AWM EZ0135)

The Germans set up a cheering and shouting ... and simultaneously charged us in mass formation ... and got in amongst us fellows ... I felt sick, then steady as a rock.

Corporal A. G. Thomas, 6th Battalion, 9 May 1916

THE SUPPORT LINES

No songs are sung and no poetry written about fatigue parties.

Private D. B. Fry, 3rd Battalion, 11 November 1916

The AIF in France was almost entirely a fighting force, trained for the front line. British soldiers provided most of the support that it required. In the British army, the ratio of men in the front line to men in the support lines was roughly 1:1. In the AIF on the Western Front the ratio was more like 20:1, meaning that about 5 per cent of AIF men were operating in the support lines. These men were playing a role in all the services — rail and light rail, depot work, headquarters, ordnance, training, engineering, communications, the divisional and the corps workshops, packhorse and wagon work, the forges, general labour and medical services.

Soldiering in the front line was by far the most dangerous occupation, as the Roll of Honour at the Australian War Memorial attests. But in the support lines there were many tasks performed by Australians within the range of the long guns. Runners routinely negotiated the hazardous route back to Battalion headquarters.

Dispatch riders with the Australian Signalling Company (ASC) carried homing pigeons in wicker baskets to trenches in the battle zones; signallers ran cable wire across perilous surfaces, and rum and ration parties braved the worst of places knowing that exhausted men, sometimes soaked to the skin, were praying for their arrival. Soldiers (and clergy) manned Australian Comfort Fund stalls, dealing coffee and tea not far from embattled trenches. The men of the mobile kitchens did the same. Light railway gangs laid tracks into hazardous territory, while others took packhorses and wagons laden with ammunition to places that light rail could not reach.

Some distance further back, more Australians were labouring in the workshops, repairing guns, trucks, water pumps and other contraptions, filling sandbags, shoeing horses, making chaff, cooking and carrying, supervising networks of communication or mountains of ordnance, or serving headquarters in manifold ways. The Australians who worked in the support lines were an integral part of the AIF on the Western Front. Those who moved constantly between the front line and the back areas probably worked harder than the fighters — the ration parties, the rum details, the signallers and the messengers had sometimes to struggle for miles under the weight of their baggage, the perils of a pocked and pulverised landscape, and the spray of enemy fire.

Of course, the stretcher-bearers are part of this story too — they are in a category all of their own.

Bayonet drill. Men of the 28th Battalion near Renescure, France, September 1917. (AWM E00684)

LEFT: A cookhouse of the 5th Australian Division unit at Vaulx. Photographed during the battle for Bullecourt, 5 May 1917. (AWM E02008)

Of all the Australian official photographs, none gained a wider publicity than this picture of the Band of the 5th Australian Infantry Brigade playing the 'Victoria March' as it passes through the Grand Place, Bapaume, on 19 March 1917. The image was widely regarded as characteristic of the fine fighting spirit that animated the Australian troops in the dramatic events of that period. The ruins of the town are still smouldering. A few miles away, on the Lagnicourt–Noreuil line, the fighting continues. (AWM E00426)

Nice quiet day. Packed up belongings and relieved 19th [Battalion]. Battle in support trenches. Plenty of fatigue here. Engineering by day and ration carrying at night from road to Front Line.

Sergeant D. E. MacDonald, 17th Battalion, 8 May 1916

Officers of the 6th Australian Infantry Brigade in their billets at the 'Catacombs' beneath Hill 63 in the Messines sector. During the winter of 1917, from December 1917 to March 1918, the Brigade used the Catacombs as a reserve position after coming out of the front line. From here working parties were nightly sent back to the front line area for the construction of earthworks. (AWM E01509)

The Smith's Shop of the No. 6 Australian Motor Transport Company, St Leger, France, 6 August 1918. Left to right: Captain H. H. Bird; Corporal Smalley; Artificer W. Buckley, sitting; Sergeant (Sgt.) Fewster; Sgt. Reid; Artificer A. Slater; Sgt. Gamble; J. Emmerton. (AWM E02918)

RIGHT: A dispatch rider departs for the forward units with a basket of carrier pigeons, 20 March 1917. His point of departure is the Signal Office and Headquarters of the 4th Australian Divisional Signalling Company on the Vaulx-Beugny Road. (AWM E00646)

Chaffing fodder with a hand machine for the horses of the 11th Field Artillery Brigade in rest at Bailleul, prior to moving into the line at Ypres, September 1917. (AWM E00666)

All sections were busily engaged, road-making, extending light rail tracks, advancing artillery, registering the artillery fire, erecting communication lines and the thousand and one details connected with an advance ... The ammunition dumps grow and appear endless — shells — shells — millions of shells — Gad! There are enough to make a roadway to Berlin: and still they come.

Frank Hurley, 28 September 1917

The Royals with the Aussies: Cooks of B Company of the 27th Battalion with their three bunny rabbits, duckling and kitten — 'souvenired' pets, known as 'The Royal Family'. Ribemont, 25 May 1918. (AWM E02427)

We were given the task of delivering [bombs] ... I suppose the full load was about a hundredweight, and with this we had to travel about half a mile through a narrow sap, with a veritable hail of shells falling round us ... Some of the fellows dropped out, others dropped part or the whole of their load, but most of us saw the distance out, realising that the delivery of the bombs was ... life or death to the men in the line.

Lieutenant F. H. Semple, 18th Battalion, 13 August 1916

An Australian field kitchen, 24th Battalion, with a hot meal for the advancing troops, passing through the ruins in Bapaume, 19 March 1917.

(AWM E00389)

AIF mechanics. Building up motor car springs in a 1st Divisional workshop, April 1918. The state of the roads in the Wallon-Cappel area kept the mechanics busy. (AWM E02036)

LEFT: Overhauling the guns. Australian mechanics of the 24th and 29th Ordnance Mobile Workshops near Reninghelst, at work on Australian field guns after heavy firing during the Third Battle of Ypres. The 29th Ordnance Workshop was an Imperial unit, commanded at the time of the photograph by Captain Donald Ross Cameron, MC, Australian Army Ordnance Corps (AAOC). This workshop was with the Australians for more than twelve months commencing at Heilly and Varennes on the Somme, then moving on to Becordel and Bapaume. (Frank Hurley. AWM E01206)

Up 4.30am trench fatigues till midday with 30 men. Visited salient between 11 and noon. 'Snaps' taken. Bath afternoon. Showery and cold. Hailstorm.'

Sergeant D. E. MacDonald, 17th Battalion, 8 May 1916

Sergeant J. C. E. Rosengard, a sergeant cook of the 3rd Battalion, drawing rations of bread and hare from a farmhouse somewhere between Sec Bois and Borre. The farmhouse became 3rd Battalion headquarters in April 1918. Civilians in the area had fled in haste leaving many farmhouses still stocked with quantities of flour, potatoes, livestock, game and bread. (AWM E02268)

'COLD SWEAT' — THE STRETCHER-BEARERS

God help us in a scrap here, we are 4 miles from a dressing station.

Corporal A. G. Thomas, 6th Battalion, 3 November 1916

Some front line soldiers believed the stretcher-bearers were the bravest of all men in the AIF. Unarmed and upright, exposed to enemy fire, they went steadily on their way to the wounded.

Stretcher-bearers were attached to field ambulance units and belonged to the Australian Army Medical Corps (AAMC). Infantry battalions also had their own bearers, some of whom were members of the band when not on duty. Bearers carried 75 to 90 kilogram loads and more, over crater-ridden or sodden ground, or along trenches barely wide enough for a stretcher. Their knuckles tore as they edged along the trench ways. In the winters their fingers near froze onto the handles of the stretcher. In the hot months their eyes and mouths were covered with flies. At night they worked, sometimes in the full light of flares and other times in complete blackness.

Under an artillery barrage, they would routinely scurry to the site of a shell burst to attend the wounded, knowing that the most likely place for the next shell to land was the same spot or somewhere nearby. In battle zones, amid shot and shell, soldiers watched them go about their work, clear targets for sniper fire or the random scatter of shrapnel. In these conditions, the Red Cross armband was no guarantee of immunity. The knowledge that these men would not hesitate to rescue the wounded was crucial to the front line soldier's morale.

The stretcher-bearers traded safety for a degree of independence. They accepted extreme vulnerability in exchange for minimal regimentation and relief from certain hated fatigues. But the cost to their minds and their bodies was great. In July 1916, one of the bearers wrote in his diary of a day in the battle of Fromelles. Trench floors under shellfire were cluttered with dead and wounded. They lay in heaps behind the parapets, and the sound 'like a thousand iron foundries, was deafening and dreadful ...':

We crept along seeking first of all the serious cases of wounded. Backwards and forwards we travelled between the firing line and the RAP with knuckles torn and bleeding due to the narrow passageways. 'Cold sweat', not perspiration, dripped from our faces and our breath came out in gasps ... By the time we had completed two trips [each of 3 miles] ... we were ... completely exhausted.

(Private W. J. A. Allsop, 8th Field Ambulance, 20 July 1916)

Stretcher-bearers bringing out wounded of the 4th Division from the front line near Delville Wood, Longueval, France, December 1916. Their journey through rain and mud was over a distance of more than 3 kilometres. (AWM E00049)

The Stretcher-Bearers could not get the wounded out any way than over the top and across the open. They had to carry me four miles with a man waving a Red Cross flag in front and the Germans did not open fire on us.

Lieutenant H. W. Crowle, 10th Battalion, 25 August 1916

Making use of the light railway during the Somme offensive in the winter of 1917. The stretchers, bearing the wounded, were placed on these trolleys, giving patients a far more comfortable trip to the rear than by 'hand-carrying'. (AWM E00249)

A scene on the Menin Road near Hooge during the battle of 20
September 1917. The wounded on stretchers are waiting to be taken
to clearing stations; those men able to walk make their own way.
(Hurley. AWM E00711)

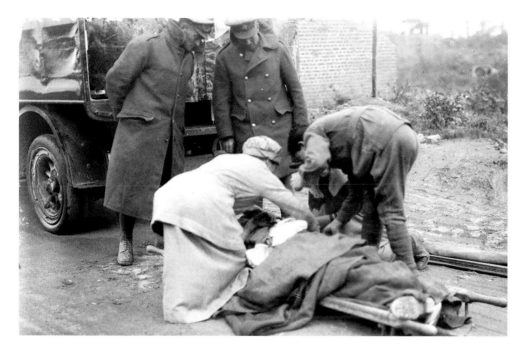

Took Watson down and returned for Alf but a shell had again got him and took both legs off: put tourniquet [on] and was bringing stretcher when a shell landed behind me and blew me down: bit through thigh and back and Morrie also got another one; lost a lot of blood and was very weak but managed to hobble out ...

Corporal William Burrell, stretcher-bearer with B Company, 17th Battalion, 20 September 1917

ABOVE: Sister Pearl E. Corkhill, MM (Military Medal), Australian Army Nursing Service (AANS). Her military medal was awarded for bravery under aerial attack at the No. 38 Casualty Clearing Station, France, 1918. Sister Corkhill was from Tilba Tilba in New South Wales. (AWM A04728)

ABOVE LEFT: An unidentified Australian nursing sister attending to a stretcher case on the road near Brie, 8 September 1918. At least 2,139 Australian nurses served abroad between 1914 and 1919, some of these in casualty clearing stations on the Western Front and many more in hospitals in France and England. (AWM E03322)

We could hear someone over towards the German entanglements calling for a stretcher-bearer; it was an appeal no man could stand against.

2nd Lieutenant S. Fraser, 58th Battalion,
31 July 1916

ABOVE: An unidentified stretcher case at an advanced dressing station of the 3rd Australian Field Ambulance, near the Menin Road at Ypres. (Hurley. AWM E00714)

LEFT: Treating the wounded at an advanced dressing station near Ypres, September 1917. (AWM E00715)

RIGHT: Gassed Australian soldiers lying in the open, close to an aid post near Bois de l'Abbe, 27 May 1918. They were gassed in operations around Villers-Bretonneux. The men are lying on the ground in their contaminated clothes, inhaling further quantities of the vapour. (AWM E04851)

I can tell you I should never have got out alive. Most of the stretcher-bearers were killed and wounded and the wounded could not get out.

Lance Corporal J. Cohen, 24th Battalion, 29 July 1916

So tired, so dead beat were they that many of them, when opportunity offered, slept the heavy drugged sleep of utter exhaustion for twenty-four hours on end. Their faded earth-stained uniforms hung loosely from bodies which had lost as much as two stone in as many months.

Lieutenant H. R. Williams, 56th Battalion, from his *Comrades of the Great Adventure* (1935), p. 289

Exhausted stretcher-bearers of the 9th Field Ambulance in the mud of a railway embankment near Zonnebeke Railway Station. They had worked for sixty hours before stopping to rest and falling asleep, oblivious to enemy shellfire. (AWM E00941)

A scene during the battle of Hamel (4 July 1918), showing American and Australian stretcher-bearers waiting near the front line after the infantry had passed. (AWM E02691)

7.11.17 (Flers): We have to carry across the open here with a white flag and Fritz does the same. The tracks are all knee-deep [in mud] in places and we have to have six on a stretcher. There is a tank close by and they are peculiar things alright.

Corporal William Burrell, MM, 17th Battalion

German prisoners near Plum Duff trench, acting as stretcher-bearers during the Battle of Messines, 7 June 1918. Corporal P. L. Roberts, 10th Field Ambulance, is second from the right. (AWM E00476)

Stretcher-bearers at work in the devastated landscape of Passchendaele, October 1917.
(AWM E001127)

FROZEN WASTES

It is no joke being in the trenches this weather ...
God knows how I am able to stand it.

(Captain F. W. Moulsdale, 7th Machine Gun Company, 17 November 1916)

The Australians' ordeal on the Somme in 1916 was followed by the worst French winter in forty years. More than 20,000 AIF men were evacuated suffering from trench foot, frostbite and exhaustion. When it rained heavily, men were compelled to stand knee-deep in waterlogged trenches sometimes for days, or they tried to sleep in 'possies' scraped out below the parapets, hoping they would not be buried alive if the sodden walls caved in.

'There was not a place anywhere in the trench where we could stand clear of water ...' wrote Lt. F. H. Semple of the 18th Battalion, in November 1916, 'as soon as I took my boots off my feet swelled rapidly so that I could not put my boots on again and I had to make my way to the ambulance station, barefooted. The distance was something like two miles.'

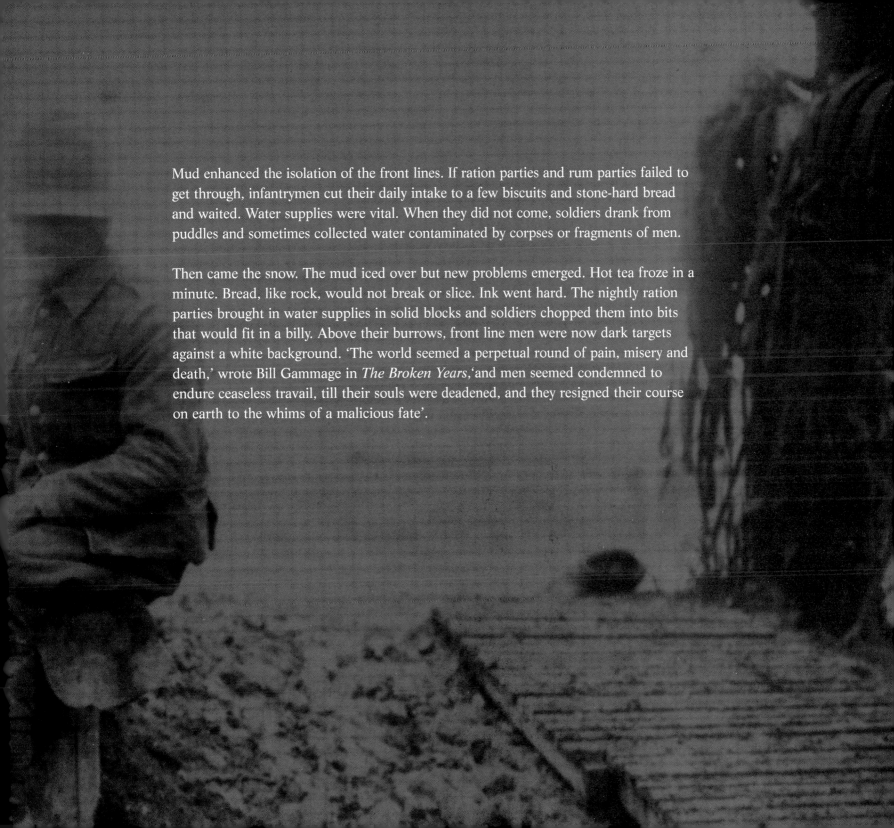

Mud enhanced the isolation of the front lines. If ration parties and rum parties failed to get through, infantrymen cut their daily intake to a few biscuits and stone-hard bread and waited. Water supplies were vital. When they did not come, soldiers drank from puddles and sometimes collected water contaminated by corpses or fragments of men.

Then came the snow. The mud iced over but new problems emerged. Hot tea froze in a minute. Bread, like rock, would not break or slice. Ink went hard. The nightly ration parties brought in water supplies in solid blocks and soldiers chopped them into bits that would fit in a billy. Above their burrows, front line men were now dark targets against a white background. 'The world seemed a perpetual round of pain, misery and death,' wrote Bill Gammage in *The Broken Years*, 'and men seemed condemned to endure ceaseless travail, till their souls were deadened, and they resigned their course on earth to the whims of a malicious fate'.

Mud from the top of our heads to the bottom of our boots, drenched to the very skin, your thoughts must be alone for the men perishing in the front line ... No songs are sung and no poetry written about fatigue parties.

Private D. B. Fry, 3rd Battalion, 11 November 1916

Australians at Montauban, France, in December 1916, cleaning the winter mud from boots and clothes. (AWM E00016)

An AIF soldier feeding an exhausted, mud-covered mule on the road at Fricourt, some time in December 1916. (AWM E00091)

The Australians' second winter on the Western Front, 1917–18, also brought appalling conditions. Persistent rain turned the battlefields of the Ypres sector in Belgium into a quagmire. Here, a mule team with supplies for the front struggles in the mud on a track near Potijze Farm.
(AWM E00963)

LEFT: Men like mules. At Bernafay, in December 1916, Australian ambulance men carry their comrades, suffering from trench foot, to a nearby transport. In the background are the Nissen huts of the 14th Field Ambulance.
(AWM E00081)

About the MUD here ... on foot one has to go very cautiously. Last time we were here one of our officers rode into a shell hole. His horse disappeared in the mud and he was only rescued with great difficulty. He had to be pulled out with ropes and in doing so they strained his internal organs.

Captain C. E. Gatliff, 13th Field Artillery Brigade, 31 December 1916

We reached the open valley and flung ourselves upon a sloping bank, oblivious of the driving rain and biting wind. This was the lowest depth to which my physical powers had ever sunk. I felt that by a slight effort of the will I could die and end it all. Our officers were in a bad way, too, and vainly strove to rally us, telling us to keep moving lest we die of exposure.

Sergeant A. A. Brunton, 3rd Anzac Light Rail, 22 November 1916

Captain Charles Bean, Official War Correspondent, shin-deep in the mud of Gird trench near Gueudecourt in France, c. December 1916. (AWM E00572)

RIGHT: Two unidentified Australian soldiers outside their 'humpy' on the Somme during the winter of 1916–17. (AWM E00045)

Whenever possible, ration parties carried hot meals in petrol tins and miscellaneous containers to men in the front lines. Here, 10th Battalion men enjoy hot stew and mugs of hot tea in the line at Eaucourt l'Abbaye, during the Somme advance of February 1917. (AWM E00252)

A sick parade at Eaucourt L'Abbaye, during the advance on the Somme in the winter of 1916–1917. 'Trench feet' was the chief complaint. One soldier has his legs enclosed in sandbags as a temporary protection against mud and damp.
(AWM E00233)

Finding an entrenching tool, I hollowed out a shelf in the side of the trench, laid my waterproof sheet on it, and lying down on it I drew my overcoat over me, and praying it would not rain again, I was soon sound asleep. When I awoke it was terribly cold ... my feet protruded from the overcoat and the caked mud on my big legging-boots was covered with a thin coating of white frost.

Lieutenant R. A. McInnes, 53rd Battalion, November 1916

Preparing hot meals. Australians at work at a 'cooker' belonging to the
2nd Battalion at Flesselles, December 1916. (AWM E00025)

At Longueval in January 1917, an Australian soldier collects a cup of water under a frozen tank.
(AWM E00171)

LEFT: In the Somme area, December 1916, Australian soldiers carrying hot stew for their unit's evening meal.
(AWM E00092)

The shell craters are filled with water and battlefield is a vast quagmire. One of the most pitiful and heroic sights is to see the ammunition packhorses bringing up shells and charges — their drivers leading and often going up to the thigh in slimy mud, the horses stumble through sometimes falling into shell craters, from which they have to be hauled. Oh, it is a wicked, agonising sight.

Frank Hurley, 23 October 1917

BILLETS AND BLIGHTIES

Tramped back from the slaughter ground to scenes of peace and grandeur. What a relief. The men soon forgot everything and they soon started into song.

Corporal A. G. Thomas, 6th Battalion, 21 August 1916

After Fromelles and Pozières in 1916, the Australians understood that war on the Western Front was, as one sergeant put it, 'a roaring boiling hell of shot and shell and mangled men'. It was clear the chance of survival was a bloody lottery. A serious wound — a 'blighty' — was now a blessing to many, an honourable way out of the battlefield. 'Many a man smiles,' wrote an officer with the field ambulance, 'when told he will never be able to fight again or that he won't be right for some months.'

The regular turnover of men in the front line also gave relief from the ordeal. A stint in the line was generally limited to three to seven days, followed by an escape to the rest areas. Men might also get temporary leave in England. Unlike Gallipoli, a complete break from the war zone was part of the in-and-out routine. Soldiers were often billeted on farms and in villages, and their lack of shyness and formality, it was said, generally made for good relations with their hosts. So too did the money in their pockets. On 'six bob a day' the Australian infantryman was the highest paid soldier in the war. The British soldier got just one bob a day.

On French farms, AIF men helped to bring in the harvest and they 'put in' with the daily chores — fetching water, feeding animals, collecting eggs and chopping wood. In the villages and towns they spent up in the cafés. They bought chocolates for local children. They were thought to be a soft touch for street peddlers — sellers of eggs or cakes or fresh fruit. And at just five francs a bottle, they acquired a taste for French champagne.

In Flanders, during the horrors of battle at Menin Road, Polygon Wood, Broodseinde Ridge and Passchendaele, the cafés or *estaminets* of reachable towns were havens for men on leave. 'After the miseries of the trenches,' wrote one of them, 'what palaces were the warm, brightly lit cafés. Here was laughter, gaiety and the sparkle of bright eyes.' Here were illustrated newspapers and Flemish beer, fire-warmed surrounds, hospitality, the reaffirmation of life.

The photography of soldiers at rest and play was a popular theme for official photographers and for the soldiers with cameras. It was not difficult or dangerous. It was an acceptable subject either for a national readership, in the case of the illustrated press, or for an anxious family waiting, somewhere in Australia, for news of their man at the Western Front.

The caption attached to this donated photograph reads: 'Anzacs in France. Machine Gunners out of the trenches. With a swinging back-to-billets step these Anzacs are leaving trench duty for their well-earned rest.' (AWM P00077.008)

RIGHT: One of the most famous of Frank Hurley's repertoire — a photograph of 1st Australian Infantry Battalion men outside their billets in the Cavalry Barracks at Ypres, following an eight-week ordeal in the trenches. Many of Hurley's photos, like this one, had an almost incandescent clarity that few other photographers could match. (Hurley. AWM E01404)

I think I will be away from the Batt. about 2 months, then I hope the war will be over. I had a terrible shaking up, though I never lost my nerve for a moment. Some of the men went mad ...

Lance Corporal J. Cohen, 24th Battalion, 29 July 1916

Taking it easy. Men of the 26th Battalion at ease on the steps of a church in a rest area behind the Somme.
(AWM E00028)

A picnic. 'Sgt. MacDonald (right), Cpl. Verrells and Pte. West ... Alongside our billet at Streaky Bacon Farm, May 1916.' (Sgt. D. E. MacDonald. Mitchell Library PXB226/137)

BELOW: Flesselles, France, December 1916. The 2nd Battalion barber, Private H. J. Sewell, at work. A haircut, like a proper shave or a hot shower, was out of the question while the men were in the trenches. (AWM E00029)

One of Gunner Barnes's many photos of soldiers, and locals, in France. Members of the 4th Divisional Ammunition Column in front of their billet at Estaires, a small town near the Western Front, June 1916. Next to the billet is possibly a *chocolaterie*. (Lent by Gunner Barnes. AWM C00443)

Monday, Monasterie ... went to 'our house' and had a good time: it makes me wish to be home once more: the girls reminded me much of Elsie and Nell: she sat on my knee and I taught her how to count in English.

Corporal William Burrell, 17th Battalion, 13 August 1917

Writing home.
Flesselles, December
1916. (AWM E00030)

The 'Shrapnels', an Australian concert party on the stage of a barn theatre at Maricourt on the Somme, January 1917. (AWM E00099)

Sunday. Set off for Cordinette about 6 miles off. These billets were small and dirty and the people very unsociable. Took their pumps to pieces etc. and made things unpleasant for us.

Sergeant D. E. MacDonald, 17th Battalion, 16 June 1916

I am off once again to France. I cannot grumble as I have had a fair rest [in England] for ten months.

Sergeant W. Rowley, 18th Battalion,
6 March 1918

A studio portrait of Sapper James West of the 3rd Australian Tunnelling Company with a French woman from Noeux Les Mines, c. 1917. The details of this friendship are unknown but more than 15,000 Australian soldiers took a wife or fiancée back to Australia. (Donated. AWM P00615.004)

Wounded AIF men in a converted chapel at Millencourt,
February 1917. (AWM E00342)

I was dead beat, and wishing to goodness something would hit me so that I could go down with a clear conscience.

Private T. J. Cleary, 17th Battalion, 5 August 1916

An Australian buying winkles (molluscs) from a French hawker in a village on the Somme where his battalion was resting during the winter of 1916–1917.
(AWM E00048)

The British official photographers visited farms and villages around Armentières to get shots of Australians relaxing in their billets or helping their hosts by doing chores. In this photo, on the edge of the manure pit, two AIF men collect water while chatting to local children — an ideal photo subject for the newspapers. (AWM EZ0036)

At last the 21st Battalion has appeared ... The barrage has lifted, and half dazed, we climb from the trenches and make a wild rush to get away while we have the chance.

Lieutenant K. S. Anderson, 22nd Battalion, 30 July 1916

'An old Frenchwoman serves coffee to six unidentified Australian and Scottish soldiers at an *estaminet* (small cafe) in her village, which is within 800 yards of the trenches in a comparatively quiet sector.' Bois-Grenier, June 1916. (AWM EZ0032)

THE SOLDIER–PHOTOGRAPHERS

Very busy indeed in town getting remaining photos and making arrangements for others to be sent on. Parcelled up snaps, albums, diaries and souvenirs etc. and registered [them] to Kitty.

Sergeant D. E. MacDonald, 17th Battalion, 24 May 1916

They were the unauthorised photographers on the Western Front, the soldiers who carried cameras and took photographs contrary to orders; who smuggled out their rolls of film in the pockets of wounded soldiers or men going on leave, and who got new film by equally tricky means. The visual record they compiled — the fraction of it that survives in archives and libraries around Australia — complements the work of the official photographers, and it differs from that work in important ways.

For a start, the soldier–photographer had the opportunity to photograph the men of his unit and their doings in some detail. He was there all the time. His shots are quirky, idiosyncratic, comic at times, artful at others, in focus, out of focus, sometimes obsessive (ruins galore, or a dozen shots of the Cloth Hall), and documentary in ways that official photographs did not address. There is a certain informality and candidness that marks the work of the soldier–photographers.

When the Australian War Museum pursued its campaign to acquire soldiers' wartime photographs in the 1920s, it did not fail to have the donors or lenders provide 'photographic descriptions' where possible. So the record is frequently one of picture and caption, and that double makes the resource all the more informative. But it is informative in ways that the official photographers might not know, or perhaps not want to know. A photo of a 35th Battalion man beside his dugout bears the caption: 'It will be noticed he has salved some bedding from a neighbouring village, vacated by the civil inhabitants.' This is first-hand detail from the everyday life of the front line soldier.

Such detail might extend beyond the khaki world of the trenches to that of the French or Belgian people around them. 'French civilians digging for buried savings among the ruins of their homes at Fricourt ...', reads the caption to one soldier's photo. The official photographers were duty-bound to follow the directions of C. E. W. Bean who was building a national record of AIF achievement, but the soldier–photographer 'shot' what he liked whenever circumstances allowed. His imagined audience was not his nation but his family, or the mates in his battalion. That further strengthened the tourist theme in his camera work. In a diary entry for 27 July 1917, Corporal William Burrell writes of his photo snaps on a route march as if they were part of a holiday sequence:

Bapaume: hot day ... packed up and moved off at 4 pm: solid march and very hot to Beaucourt: off packs and went into the Ancre for a swim: trés bien: this place has seen plenty of 'stoush' by the look of it: Got one of a ruined chateau: bivouacked but the 'skeetas were very vicious.

Got leave to go to Pozières to put a cross on Mr Haigh's friend's grave: had a good roam round and found most of the old places: still dead lying about. 'P' [photo] of 2nd Division Cross and grave of Black. Got a lift in motor transport back.

Corporal William Burrell, 17th Battalion,
12 July 1917

TOP: 'French civilians digging for buried savings among the ruins of their homes at Fricourt, after their return in June 1917.'
(Lent by Cpl. W. Baird. AWM C04211)

LEFT: 'Lt. Bob Purcell, MC, 35th Battalion, outside his dugout in the Villers reserve line. It will be noticed he has salved some bedding from a neighbouring village, vacated by the civil inhabitants to escape the Germans, during the enemy advance in March, 1918.'
(Lent by Lt. H. S. Wyndham, AWM C04095)

'A party of 6th Australian Infantry Brigade working with engineers
burying a cable near Villers-Bretonneux, July 1918.'
(Lent by Cpl. Lock. AWM C4882)

Sunday. Church parade 10.30. Afternoon looked through Town Hall and then short while in cathedral listening to organ. Took several snaps while out.

Sergeant D. E. MacDonald, 17th Battalion, 3 September 1916

'Some members of the Chinese Labour Corps, with men of the 2nd Australian Light Railway Operating Coy, in Belgium during October 1917.'

(Lent by Captain Williams. AWM C01358)

'A tank passing through the ruins of Ypres in October 1917.'
(Lent by Captain Williams. AWM C1392)

'Gunners of the 102nd Howitzer Battery outside their dugout at the battery position, near Hermes, June 1917.' The roof of the dugout is camouflaged with netting, while the front is 'armoured' with sheets of corrugated iron.

(Lent by Gunner Barnes. AWM C00439)

'Some enemy machine guns and trench mortars captured by the 13th Battalion during the battle of Hamel, 4 July 1918. The trophies were photographed at Hamel before being sent to base.'

(Lent by Private Cook. AWM C1749)

Saturday, July 7. Reveille 4 am: stretcher drill during morn: sleep in afternoon. Roam around Bapaume after tea. Went into the vault under the ruined cathedral and seen the skulls: there are hundreds of them and the talk is that they are those of the victims of the French Revolution.

Corporal William Burrell, 17th Battalion, 7 July 1917

'The remains of the church at Bapaume. The Australians in this photo have just discovered the entrance to the crypt, in which so many skulls were found when the Australians first entered Bapaume in March 1917.' (Lent by Sgt. S. S. Varley. AWM C4692)

6th Sat. May ... letter writing most of the day ... church service after tea very nice. Snaps taken.

Sergeant D. E. MacDonald, Diary, 6 May 1916

'This house was occupied by the 3rd Australian Divisional DADOS. It is situated on the Amiens–Albert Road and is well known by the warning on the wall, viz: "Pessimists shot on sight", which was written just after the British retirement on the Somme.' (Lent by Warrant Officer Batteye. AWM C4550)

'The betting ring at the 4th Australian Divisional Race Meeting at Allonville, France, in July 1918.' (Lent by Private Cook. AWM C1747)

Walked to Weymouth after tea and bought Xmas cards and also got my films and prints: not too bad.

Sergeant William Burrell, MM (Military Medal), on leave in England, 17 October 1917

'A group of dispatch riders of the 3rd Divisional Signal Company, Australian Engineers, at Foucaucourt, in January 1919.' (Lent by Cpl. A. F. Hollins. AWM C4824)

RIGHT: An officer's artistry. 'A silhouette showing the destruction of the railway line between Mons and Avenes. The line has since been repaired. November 1918.' (Lent by Lt.-Col. G. F. Murphy, CMG, DSO. AWM C4883)

HURLEY —
LEGENDARY MAN

*Once this must have been a glorious spot in summer.
Death alone now dwells here.*

Frank Hurley, 1917

The first Australians to be appointed as official photographers were Frank Hurley and Hubert Wilkins. They arrived on the Western Front in the middle of 1917. Hurley was there for about four months, after which he departed for Palestine. Wilkins stayed on.

Charles Bean described Frank Hurley as 'a rare mixture of the genuine, highly sensitive artist and keen commercial man'. It was these combined talents that prompted Bean to make Hurley responsible for the publicity side of official photography, and to allow the steady, meticulous Wilkins to build up a record of men, places and events that could be relied on for photographic evidence. These differing briefs are obvious in the work of each man, for Hurley's photography reveals a flair and artistry that Wilkins did not pursue. Yet, often enough, purpose is lost in the outcome — many of Hurley's photographs are valuable historical documents while Wilkins' pictures are sometimes quite striking images.

The idea that Hurley produced a show while Wilkins' produced still picture records is perhaps too simple, but not entirely unfair. Wilkins followed Bean's orders to the letter and stuck with the job of systematically documenting one AIF-related subject after another until the end of the war on 11 November 1918. Hurley, on the other hand, was always thinking about his next show. He left the Western Front for Palestine in November 1917 and he was back in London, promoting his first war photos exhibition, sponsored by Kodak, five months before the armistice. Then he headed south. On the day that the war ended, Hurley and his new wife, Antoinette, arrived in Sydney. There he began work on his film *With the Australians in Palestine*. He was a great self-publicist. He exhibited, he lectured, he spoke at film screenings, public gatherings and luncheons. As both artist and commercial man, he was unstoppable.

His time on the Western Front in 1917 coincided almost exactly with the Third Battle of Ypres in Flanders (31 July–6 November), an offensive that cost the AIF dearly — 38,093 men killed or wounded. Hurley's diaries express his horror at the frightful slaughter that he witnessed. His photos capture the resilience of the fighters but also the desolation of faces and landscapes. He was convinced the single lens camera could never do justice to what these brave men had faced and endured.

Hurley believed, rightly, that the AIF's achievements in battle were under-represented in the pictorial coverage of the war and he was determined to boost their presence in the illustrated newspapers of England and Australia. He was the ideal man for the job. His artistry made him a fabulous press photographer — and eventually a legend. Yet if his pictures made good propaganda, they also carried an undercurrent — a style and a feeling that suggested his burning sense of the futility of this slaughter.

Australians on their way to take up front line positions in the Ypres
sector, Belgium, 25 October 1917. In the background are the ruins of
the twelfth-century Cloth Hall. (Hurley. AWM E04612)

The indispensable meat mincer, metaphor for the war itself. Cooks of
the 2nd Battalion preparing bully beef rissoles for the evening mean at
Ypres. The eternal 'bully' was turned into a variety of dishes.
(Hurley. AWM E01064)

I quickly forget the horrible doings of the day, and after a good dinner, develop my photos and then turn in.

Captain Frank Hurley, 4 October 1917

Hurley commonly sought artistic effect by framing photographs with the outline of ruins. Here motor and horse transport pass through Vlamertinghe, near Ypres. Six Australian companies routinely used the cobbled road from Poperinghe to Ypres; slower vehicles moving in a single column hug the kerb leaving the centre of the road free for faster traffic. (Hurley. AWM E00872)

RIGHT: Pioneers of the 1st Australian Division preparing a duckboard track over the muddy waste near Zonnebeke, in the Ypres sector, the day after the Australian attack on Broodseinde Ridge, 5 October 1917. (Hurley. AWM E00837)

Trademark Hurley — a view, in silhouette, of Australian artillery
limbers loaded with ammunition proceeding along the Ypres Road.
The paradox of many Hurley photographs was the extraordinary
beauty he created from landscapes of war. (Hurley. AWM E00829)

Australians acquired a reputation for being trophy collectors. Private J. Hines, A Company, 45th Battalion, was well known for his acquisitions and his trades. Here he poses with souvenirs obtained during the advance of the 4th and 13th Brigades at Polygon Wood during the Third Battle of Ypres, 27 September 1917.
(Hurley. AWM E00822)

I have tried, and tried again, to include events on a single negative but the results have been hopeless. Everything is on such a wide scale ... Figures scattered, atmosphere dense with haze and smoke — shells that simply would not burst when required.

Captain Frank Hurley, 1917

I'm sick of being almost killed or wounded and hearing that hellish din of cannonade, and dodging shells ... We have an even worse time than the infantry ...

Captain Frank Hurley, 1917

A Hurley? This is one of the many official photographs for which the documentation identifying the photographer was lost. But it was taken on 3 October 1917, when Hurley was on the Western Front and the two soldiers posed and perfectly silhouetted in the shell-crater water amid the ruins of Ypres are consistent with Hurley's artistry. (AWM E00707)

OPPOSITE: A scene on the Menin Road beyond Ypres. (Hurley. AWM E00700)

Still life posed for Hurley. Three members of the 10th Mobile Ordnance Workshop at Steenvoorde, forging a piece of steel for the repair of a heavy howitzer, 2 October 1917. (Hurley. AWM E01221)

There is no lack of darkrooms in these dingy abodes.

Captain Frank Hurley, 2 September 1917

After lunch we took the cameras through the ruins out by the Menin Gate and along the ramparts ... I took some photographs from the Post Office which have since developed successfully.

Captain Frank Hurley, 4 September 1917

View from within the Cloth Hall.
(Hurley. AWM E01230)

WILKINS — FORGOTTEN HERO

Wilkins was with the men of the 6th Brigade as they charged the summit on 1 September [1918]

Ross McMullin, *Will Dyson*

Hubert Wilkins was a country boy from South Australia who became, in quick succession, an electrical engineer, a cinematographer, a pioneer aviator, a polar explorer and a war cameraman. His life, like Hurley's, was a string of adventures. He was with the Stefansson expedition in the Arctic in 1916 when he got news of the war. He returned to London, hoping to join the Australian Flying Corps (AFC), but was rejected due to colour blindness. Charles Bean snapped him up. Wilkins became the second official photographer and travelled to the Western Front with Bean and Hurley in July 1917.

While Hurley was there, the two men followed a similar routine. They were billeted not far from the front. Each morning they said goodbye to Wilkins' flea-bitten dog and went off into the front lines or the rear lines or wherever Bean might direct them. They went as far as they could by car, then moved about on foot. Their 'camera lumper' carried a heavy pack of about 50 glass slides ('single darks'), each in a wooden frame, ready to load and shoot. They worked long days and at night returned to their billets where they proceeded to develop their negatives in a temporary darkroom, finally getting to bed after midnight, then up and out before dawn to capture the early light.

Wilkins' bravery in the front line was well known to his contemporaries. He repeatedly risked his life in battle zones. He refused to carry a firearm. His second combat award was for bravery well beyond the call of photographic duty — he came upon a disoriented platoon of American soldiers, rallied them and led them back into battle.

Tracking Wilkins' wartime oeuvre is a tricky business. At the beginning of 1918 he was joined by another six official photographers, appointed from the ranks of the AIF. But the paperwork identifying the shots taken by each photographer has been lost, so most of Wilkins' photos from that year cannot be singled out. The same misfortune applies to the period when Hurley and Wilkins were working together in 1917, though a reasonable number of Hurley pictures have since been identified — by Hurley himself, by historians and researchers. Fortunately there was a period when Wilkins was the only official photographer working on the Western Front. After Hurley left for Palestine late in 1917, Wilkins worked alone for a period of six weeks. The official photographs in this chapter are mostly from those six weeks, the aftermath of Passchendaele, 17 November to 31 December 1917.

It was winter. Christmas and the New Year were closing in. Wilkins was working on yesterday's battlefields or else in the rear lines or the towns where reserve troops were resting. He was documenting the AIF, ticking off his subjects as he went: heroic aviator, captured plane, surgery, battlefield wastelands, soldiers' billets, officers' quarters, nurses taking tea, a view of ruins, workshops, barbed-wire entanglements, a battalion parade, ruined German pillboxes, headquarters, a regimental printing office, and near endless group portraits of AIF men.

The 6oth Battalion on parade in a snow-covered field at Beussent,
20 December 1917. (Wilkins. AWM E01427)

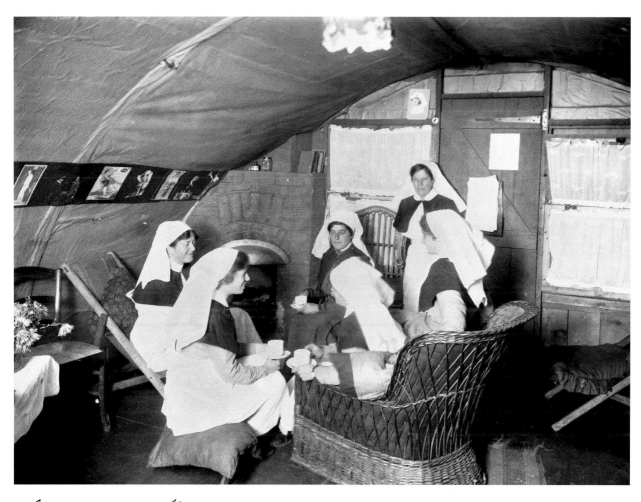

Australian nurses taking tea in their quarters at the 2nd Australian Casualty Clearing Station, near Steenwerck, 30 November 1917. Left to right: Sister Crocke Brown, Sister (Topsy) Tyson, Sister Homan (centre), Sister Louisa Storo (centre foreground), Sister Steward (standing); Sister Shepherd. An array of magazine posters, including a bathing beauty, can just be made out on the wall. (Wilkins. AWM E01280)

Lieutenant Wilkins was charged with obtaining an accurate and complete record of the fighting and other activities of the A.I.F.

Charles Bean, *The Photographic Record of the War*

The 'Anzac Coves' Concert Party in a theatre erected at Steenwerck in France, 23 November 1917. Identified left to right, standing: Private (Pte.) Reade, Pte. Ross, Pte. Gibb, Gunner Williams, Sergeant (Sgt.) Davey, Lance Corporal (LCpl.) Crossley. Sitting: LCpl. Shaw, Pte. Roberts, Sgt. Cannon, Driver Donovan (at the piano). (Wilkins. AWM E01307)

Voting for Conscription. Men of the 3rd Battalion voting in the second Conscription Referendum at Halinghen, near Samer, 8 December 1917. The referendum at the front came soon after the appalling slaughter at Passchendaele. This time the 'No' majority at home and among the troops was greater than it had been in the 1916 referendum. (Wilkins. AWM E01440)

RIGHT: Posting the proclamation of the second Australian Referendum on Conscription in the French village of Fletre, 1 December 1917. Member of the Headquarters Guard of the 1st Anzac Corps stand by. (Wilkins. AWM E01443)

Fresh cut wood. The field kitchen of the 3rd Battalion in a rest billet at Halinghen, France, on 8 December 1917. (Wilkins. AWM E01542)

Under camouflage. Restocking the gunpits of the 104th Battery during
the Australian occupation of the Ploegsteert Sector in Belgium,
December 1917. (Wilkins. AWM E01387)

The rarest of photographs — the cameraman among his shattered subjects. Here Frank Hurley poses for Wilkins among exhausted, wounded and dead Australians at Broodseinde Ridge, 12 October 1917. (Wilkins. From a print held by the National Library of Australia. MS2721)

I sometimes wonder if Wilkins is really trying to get killed.

Will Dyson, c. 11 October 1918

One of the hundreds of group portraits taken by Hubert Wilkins in the winter of 1917. Officers and men of the 3rd Pioneer Battalion on parade in the town square in Nieppe, northern France, 13 December 1917. (Wilkins. AWM E04502)

The printing office of the 23rd Battalion near Locre, Belgium, December 1917. The regimental journal was produced in this small building. The soldiers to the left seem to be holding a printing plate and a page of the journal. The tiny printing press is on the box between these two. (Wilkins. AWM E01422)

Troops of the 2nd Australian Division at 'Hyde Park Corner' near the
entrance to the Catacombs at Hill 63, in the Messines sector, 26
December 1917. (Wilkins. AWM E01588)

Wilkins was on the top of the trench all the time, getting photographs until some German at very long range sent over two sniping bullets at him which added just the touch of realism needed.

Vance Palmer, Australian Press contingent, 31 May 1918

Ahead of the front line. Wilkins was well known for his daring. Here he has raced ahead, past the bodies of dead Germans, to get a photograph of Australian infantry of the 1st Division moving forward after a tank had eliminated a line of German resistance, 9 August 1918. (Wilkins. AWM E02878)

Australians going in to battle at Mont St Quentin, 1 September 1918. Wilkins went with them. He got a photograph of the men going over the top and then went in with the second wave of attacking troops. He was the only member of the War Record's circle to be awarded military honours — he was awarded the Military Cross and Bar in June and September 1918 for assisting wounded men and for rallying American troops in battle. (Wilkins. AWM E03104)

Wilkins was with the men of the Sixth Brigade as they charged the summit on 1 September 1918.

Ross McMullin, *Will Dyson* (1984), p.173

1918: 'WE FIGHT IN OPEN FIELDS ...'

The fighting was much more to our liking than anything previously.

Sergeant C. C. Serjeant, 14th Battalion, 6 May 1918

T he offensive in Flanders around Ypres was stalled in a quagmire of mud and blood late in 1917. In the east, Russian forces surrendered, freeing up more German divisions to fight on the Western Front. The French army was reeling from a severe bout of mutinies. The New Year looked grim.

British lines were stretched thin. In March 1918 they gave way under the might of a huge German offensive along a 44-mile (70-kilometre) front. The line at the Somme near Péronne was smashed, then the line at Bapaume, and more. It seemed the war might be lost.

Between March and July 1918, the Australian divisions played a part in stemming the onslaught. They were now called the Australian Corps and were united under one command. They were rushed south to the Somme. At Hébuterne and Hangar Wood and other places, they ground the Germans to a halt. At Villers-Bretonneux near the vital rail junction of Amiens, the 13th and 15th Brigades drove the enemy back. The casualties were heavy, but nothing like 1917, and now success was with the Australians wherever they fought. The dead were many but morale was up.

This style of warfare suits us better and the men are keen and in excellent health …
We fight in open fields among hedges and farm houses and dig trenches all over the
country. We have got right away from fixed trench warfare. (Lt. Harry Hedgley, 1st Battalion)

In June, an Australian general took command of the Corps. He was John Monash. His timing was fortunate. Six weeks after his appointment, French divisions and the newly arrived Americans attacked the enemy at Soissons and brought the German offensive to an end. Charles Bean called it 'the turning point of the Great War'. Monash now applied his considerable planning skills to the Allied counteroffensive that would bring victory later in the year. Over three months of fighting, at Hamel, Mont St Quentin, Péronne and elsewhere, the Australians won stunning victories. In September they broke into the Hindenburg Line, the last German defence system.

By October, Australian battalions had been fighting for six months without interruption. They were depleted, battered and exhausted. They could do no more. Nearly 27,000 men had been killed or wounded since 8 August. Not one battalion could muster more than a quarter of its complement. Some battalions had fewer than 100 men, a tenth of full strength. On 6 October the last of the Australian divisions in the field, the Second, was withdrawn from the Western Front. The Armistice followed on 11 November 1918.

On the eve of the assault on Mont St Quentin, a line of 56th Battalion men move into place as part of General Monash's battle plan, 31 August 1918. (AWM E03201)

Away we charged yelling like devils right into His Trenches. Fritzey Bolted & we after Him I was directly after my officer and a couple Dodged Into a Dugout. We Fed Them on Bombs etc. & on To the next … I got a Bonzer coat … also a Fritz rifle.

Sergeant G. H. Molesworth, 35th Battalion, 6 March 1918

August 1918. Lieutenant Rupert Frederick Arding Downes, MC, addressing his platoon from B Company, 29th Battalion, during a rest in the advance to Harbonnieres, the battalion's second objective. In the background, the countryside is obscured by the fog of heavy shellfire. (AWM E02790)

Members of the 1st Division in support trenches at Mologhein Farm, a position situated near Strazeele Railway Station, in northern France. The locality was the scene of aggressive guerilla warfare and sharp fighting by the Australians in April 1918. (AWM E04750)

A day after the battle for Mont St Quentin, Australians lie dead amid tangles of barbed wire, 2 September 1918. Men of the 53rd Battalion had gone forward in the face of heavy machine gun fire. (AWM E03149)

Since 27 March [1918] the Australians had opposed thirty-nine enemy divisions, nineteen more than once. They defeated all, and forced six to disband. They took 29,144 prisoners, 23 per cent of the British total, 338 guns (23 per cent), and 40 miles of ground (21 per cent) ... yet they made up less than 10 per cent of the British Army.

Bill Gammage, *The Broken Years*
(Penguin, 1987), p. 204

Lieutenant General Sir John Monash, KCB, VD, Australian Corps Commander (seated), with his two Aides-de-Camp (ADC) and the Camp Commandant, at the Australian Corps Headquarters. Left to right: Captain (Capt.) A. M. Moss, ADC; Major W. W. Berry, Camp Commandant; and Capt. P. W. Simsonson, ADC. (AWM E03186)

Pilots and their Sopwith Camels at Clairmarais, 16 June 1918. Officers of C Flight, No. 4
Squadron, Australian Flying Corps (AFC) in full flying gear. Left to right: Lieutenant (Lt.) R. C.
Nelson, Lt. E. C. Crosse, Lt. G. S. Jones-Evans, Captain Edgar James McCloughry, Lt. E. V.
Culverwell, Lt. V. G. M. Sheppard, Lt. R. H. Yondale, Lt. J. C. F. Wilkinson. (AWM E02655)

LEFT: Soldiers of the 51st Battalion under the hot showers at the 5th Australian Divisional Bath
House at Daours, 21 May 1918. (AWM E02314)

We were well out in the open ... suddenly crash and several big *musher* [high-explosive] shells shrieked about our ears, then on they came thick and heavy and what was more disastrous gas two sniffs and I was satisfied ... I whipped out my helmet and jammed the rubber into my mouth put the nose clip on and then speedily warned my platoon to put on their equipment ... We have a lot of new men and they completely lost their heads, an easy thing to do when new but it is fatal in these big gassing stunts.

Corporal A. G. Thomas, 6th Battalion, 20 March 1918

The 26th Battery of Australian Field Artillery going into action near Gressaire Wood, to support the attack by the 9th Australian Infantry Brigade at Bray and Happy Valley. Identified in the foreground, left to right, are: Driver (Dvr.) E. P. Smith, Dvr. J. P. Allen and Dvr. C. Mathews. (AWM E03123)

The 108th Howitzer Battery in action at Bray, 26 August 1918. The Battery was supporting the troops of the 3rd Australian Division who were engaged in the sector beyond Suzanne. (AWM E03114)

August 1918. Infantry of the 15th Infantry Brigade, having waited two hours after the capture of their first objective, are here advancing over a hill near Warfusee-Abancourt, in pursuit of the retreating enemy. The artillery at the bottom of the hill awaits orders to move into position. (AWM E02791)

September 1918. Troops of D Company, 45th Battalion, nearing the
Hindenburg Line, the last German defence system. They are
photographed here sniping the retreating enemy who were also under
shellfire from Australian artillery. It was now possible for the
photographers (possibly Wilkins in this case) to move with the fighters
across open country. (AWM E03260)

*Knees knocked when the barrage opened
but after the start all trepidation
vanished. Wonderful barrage put up,
ground shrapnel shell on explosion lit
up the scene and we caught glimpses of
Fritz going for life.*

Private F. W. Roberts, 21st Battalion, 4 July 1918

Near Hargicourt, France, 1 October 1918.
Australian soldiers searching their German
prisoners for souvenirs after an attack on the
Hindenburg Line. (E03919)

What you might find in a German soldier's wallet — a portrait of his children. This photograph was taken from a member of the crew of a railway gun captured near Harbonnieres, France, on 8 August 1918. The Australian soldier who 'souvenired' the photo wrote on the back of it: 'A souvenir like this I think helps us to remember that there is another side to war …' Germans, of course, found similar mementos in the pockets of Australian prisoners. (AWM P00167.002)

RIGHT: Nearing the end. The Wireless Section of the 3rd Australian Divisional Signal Company marching through the streets of Péronne having departed the front line on 2 October 1918. Here an American Division, on its way to the front, looks on. Two days later, after the 2nd Division crashed through the Hindenburg defences, the entire Australian front passed to the 2nd American Corps and the Australian Corps moved to a rest area behind Amiens. Artillery units fought on, as did Australian airmen, until the Armistice on 11 November 1918. (AWM E03501)

COUNTING THE COST

'Skulls and bones and torn uniforms... lying about everywhere.'

From Charles Bean's diary, Armistice Day, 11 November 1918

Of the 61,720 Australian soldiers who died on active service in World War I, 46,319 were lost on the Western Front. Approximately 18,000 of these have no known grave. The number wounded tallied 152,171. Approximately 5,750 more were gassed. Many of the survivors, wounded or otherwise, died young.

The official photographers and the soldier–photographers shared a common interest in subjects, such as men in the lines, guns, equipment, ruins, trophies, devastated landscapes and battlefield graves. They also shared responsibility for the two great deficiencies in the record — they were unable to 'capture' much action and they avoided coverage of the dead en masse. The official cameramen were almost certainly told not to cover this subject, while the soldier–photographers might not have had the chance, or the inclination, to record death so legion. Statistics tell us that battle after battle concluded with a carnage that could be measured by the hectare or even the square mile. So too does written testimony. The surviving photo collections contain the occasional photograph of one, two or three bodies, usually the enemy dead, but rarely is this scale exceeded. Some will put this down to contemporary standards of decency or respect for the dead. But for the official record it was a breach of Bean's pledge to document the AIF experience as completely as possible.

Words also obscure the cost. Statistics speak of 'dead and wounded'. Neither of these categories confront the reality or the scale of horrific mutilation. 'Wounded' simply does not have the power to represent what happened, physically *and* mentally, to so many soldiers.

But photographers on the Western Front (1916–1918) did register something of the cost of war. It can be seen, for example, in some of Hurley's pictures — in the blank, shell-shocked stare of soldiers waiting for treatment in the dressing stations. It is there in the discreet photographs of men, with their padre, standing quietly around an open grave. It is there, so poignantly, in the photo portraits of men who never came home. The cost of war is evident in the cluttered images of battlefield cemeteries where the earth is fresh-turned, the graves lumpy and disorderly, some so close together the crosses almost touch, others scattered around impediments such as shell holes and metal wreckage (*les vestiges de guerre*). Disinterment, reburial, landscaping, lawns, headstones — all that would come later, after the war. The power of these wartime photographs thus comes from the immediacy of their taking. Landscaping and orderliness, like that word 'wounded', obscures so much.

Of those men lost forever in the mud of Flanders or the bomb craters of France, or in collapsed dugouts, or in trenches that buckled and folded over them, asphyxiated and entombed them — the 18,000 men with no known grave — we can only wonder.

Studio portrait made in Egypt of Gunner (later Bombardier) Thomas George Herweg, 1st Brigade Australian Field Artillery. Bombardier Herweg died of wounds in France on 7 October 1918. He has no known grave and his name is commemorated on a Memorial Panel at the Bronfray Farm Military Cemetery, Bray-Sur-Somme, France.

(Donated. AWM P02905.008)

Aboriginal serviceman, Cpl. Harry Thorpe, MM. Wounded in action at Pozières in 1916 and again at Bullecourt in 1917. Conspicuous for his courage and leadership at Broodseinde near Ypres in October 1917, he was awarded the Military Medal for his 'splendid example'. Thorpe was a stretcher-bearer. On 9 August 1918 he was shot in the stomach and killed. He is buried in Heath cemetery near Harbonnieres in France.

(Donated. AWM P01695.002)

Studio portrait made in Egypt of Warrant Officer Class I Arnold Pringle, Regimental Sergeant Major, 14th Battalion, died of wounds in France, 16 October 1917.

(Donated photo. AWM P01466.001)

Studio portrait made in Brisbane, c. 1914, of Bombadier Kenneth Taylor, 11th Field Artillery Brigade (on left), killed in France, 30 December 1916, with his brother.
(Donated. AWM P00117.040)

Studio portrait made in Yass, c. 1915, of Pte. Malcolm McIntosh Southwell, 20th Battalion, killed in action on the Somme, 15 November 1916.
(Donated. AWM P00124.001)

*I only hope I have the luck to return home and
if I don't well my name will be on the Scroll of
Fame and you will be able to hold up your head
proudly with other Mothers who have lost their
noble son.*

Corporal W. D. Gallwey, 47th Battalion, 3 March 1917

A soldier's photo of a cemetery near Pozières showing Australian and German graves side by side.
(Donated by Cpl. Lock. AWM C04892)

LEFT: Capt. Thomas Baker, Australian Flying Corps. Baker's flying career lasted just four months. In that time he was credited with destroying eight enemy planes and forcing down another four. He was shot out of the sky on 4 November 1918, one week before the Armistice. He is buried in the communal cemetery at Escanaffles in Belgium. He was from Smithfield in South Australia.
(Donated. AWM H12861)

Dozens and dozens [of dead] ... all distorted and frozen looks of horror on their faces.

Captain A. J. Cunningham, MC, 2nd Field Company, 27 July 1916

A padre reads the burial service beside the grave of an Australian soldier who died in a casualty clearing station nearby.

(Donated. AWM P00077.011)

The premonition that I had when leaving Sydney, that I would never see home again still hangs about me.

Private E. O. Neaves, 20th Battalion, 15 February 1917. Killed in action 6 November 1917

[Going] to Fromelles to get some photos before the place changes ... Simply full of our dead ... skulls and bones and torn uniforms ... lying about everywhere ... a misty drizzle ...

From Charles Bean's diary, Armistice Day, 11 November 1918. (The photos Bean sought have not been found.)

An uncommon photograph for an Australian official photographer. Bodies of troops — in this case American troops laid out near Gillemont Farm, 3 October 1918, with an open mass grave in the background. (AWM E04942P)

A German machine gunner lying dead at his post in a trench near
Hargicourt, 9 September 1918. (AWM E03351)

Australian Engineers of the 15th Field Company making crosses for their dead comrades amid the ruins of Ypres. They used oak taken from the ruins of the Cloth Hall. (AWM E01405)

RIGHT: Fitting an artificial limb at No. 2 Australian Auxiliary Hospital, Southall, England, 22 May 1919. (AWM D00571)

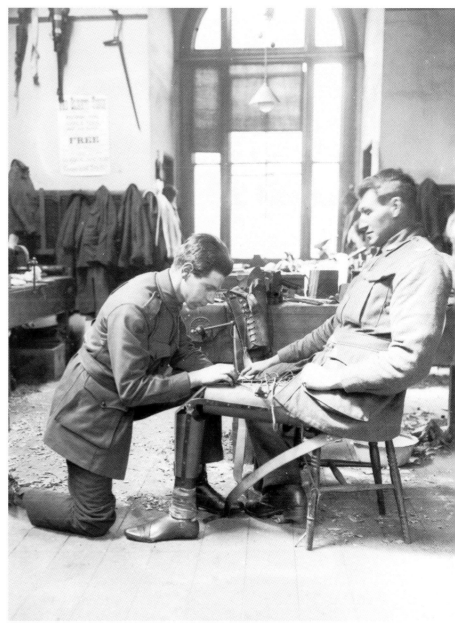

One of our Lieuts got shell shock and he literally cried like a child; some that I saw carried down out of the firing line were struggling and calling out for their mother, while others were blabbering sentences that one could not make out.'

Lieutenant L. J. Martin, 1st Machine Gun Battalion, 31 July 1916

Two unidentified soldiers reading inscriptions on the crosses at the cemetery at Vlamertinghe, near Ypres, 3 October 1917. (Hurley. AWM E00847)

RIGHT: Adelaide Cemetery, Villers-Bretonneux, France, 26 August 1919. French children tending graves of Australians killed in battle on the Western Front. (AWM E05925)

God be with you. Love for all Time ... Remember me to baby when she is Born — if a Boy don't make him a tin soldier but should war break out, let him enlist and do his bit if not he'll be no son of mine.

Captain A. McLeod, 16th Battalion, 9 August 1916

Frank Hurley's photographic tribute to the anonymous heroes of the
AIF, Ypres sector, 5 October 1917. (Hurley. AWM E00833)

NOTES

Pages vii–xii: Charles Bean discusses war photography in his preface to *The Photographic Record of the War*, (eds C. E. W. Bean and H. S. Gullett), Angus & Robertson, Sydney, 1923. My main source of information for the British official photographers is Jane Carmichael, *First World War Photographers*, Routledge, London, 1989.

Pages x–xiv: Bean's quest for a comprehensive photographic record is discussed in Michael McKernan, *Here is Their Spirit. A History of the Australian War Memorial, 1917-1990*, University of Queensland Press/AWM, St Lucia, 1991, pp. 53–61

Pages xiii–xv: My sources for Frank Hurley include *Hurley at War: the Photographs and Diaries of Frank Hurley in Two World Wars*, Fairfax Library, Sydney, 1986. (Introduction written by Daniel O'Keefe); also, Lennard Bickel, *In Search of Frank Hurley*, Macmillan, Melbourne, 1980. Hubert Wilkins' story is pieced together from various fragments. Something of his Western Front activity can be gleaned from Michael McKernan, *Here is Their Spirit*. Bean's *Gallipoli Mission*, AWM, Canberra, 1952, chapter 2, is also helpful, as is Ross McMullin, *Will Dyson. Cartoonist, etcher and Australia's finest war artist*, Angus & Robertson, London, 1984.

Pages xv–xix: The idea of the soldier-tourist is discussed by Richard White, 'The Soldier as Tourist: The Australian Experience of the Great War', *War and Society*, volume 5, no. 1, May 1987. The case for the importance of unauthorised soldier photography has been put together from primary sources at the Australian War Memorial (AWM) and the Mitchell Library (ML): the C and J Series caption books and corresponding soldier-photo collections are held at the AWM, and the photo albums of Sergeant D. E. MacDonald and Private D. Jackson at ML. MacDonald's diary is also held at the ML, as are the diaries and photo album of Corporal (later Sgt) William Henry Burrell. Burrell's photograph of the French woman with her sheep is no. 46 in his album. The comparison of the Cloth Hall with shops in Sydney is from the photo album of Cpl. J. M. Hamilton held at the ML.

There is one excellent website on this subject called 'Jack Turner's War', covering the experience of a Canadian soldier-photographer on the Western Front: http://collections.ic.gc.ca/turner/index.html Turner's testimony provides rare evidence of the means of clandestine photography — how film and developing 'powders' were acquired, darkroom practice and so on.

Pages xix–xx: The Kodak exhibition catalogue is a Mitchell Library item: *Catalogue of an Exhibition of War Photographs by Capt. F. Hurley … held at Kodak Salon*, Sydney, 1919. Colart's Studios marketed AWM (official) photos in the 1920s and was the AWM's darkroom for a time. A copy of the 'Digger artists' photographic exhibition catalogue is held by the AWM and the ML.

Page xxi: The lantern slide collections are held at the AWM, as are a small number of transcripts of lantern slide lectures. The finest book on the subject of remembrance after the war is Ken Inglis, *Sacred Places. War Memorials in the Australian Landscape*, Miegunyah Press, Melbourne, 1998. Still the premier narrative of Australians on the Western Front is Bill Gammage's classic, *The Broken Years* (Penguin), first published in 1974. The popular appeal of photography in relation to history and family is discussed in Roland Barthes, *Camera Lucida*, Flamingo, London, 1984.

ACKNOWLEDGMENTS

I am indebted to Ian Affleck at the Australian War Memorial for so generously sharing his time and his expertise with me, and for drawing my attention to the importance of Hubert Wilkins. I am also grateful for critical advice and assistance from Richard White (University of Sydney), Dr Peter Stanley (AWM) and Dr Suzanne Rickard. At the National Library of Australia, Margy Burn, Graeme Powell and Linda Grom helped with a successful search. Others who helped along the way were Fiona Jeffery (State Library of Victoria), Alan Davies, Arthur Easton, Judy Nelson, Jo Searle and Linda West (State Library of NSW), and Dr Phillip Deery (Victoria University, Melbourne). It has been a pleasure to publish again with ABC Books. Special thanks to my commissioning editor, Jill Brown, to my editors, Jenny Mills and Susan Morris-Yates, and to designer Melanie Feddersen.

SERIES DESCRIPTION

A: Copy negatives taken from prints lent by soldiers or their next of kin. These cover all topics and are contemporaneous with the C series.

B: Australian official photographs taken in Egypt, Palestine, etc. These also contain some small sets, lent or donated, that were taken by soldiers and nurses.

E: Photographs taken by Australian official photographers in France and Belgium. The Australian War Memorial holds half-plate and whole-plate glass negatives.

EZ: Photographs taken by British official photographers in France and Belgium prior to the appointment of the Australian official photographers, Hurley and Wilkins.

C: Original negatives lent to the Australian War Memorial by soldiers, relatives or others for copying. The War Memorial retains its half-plate copies as glass negatives. Caption books were compiled for this series.

J: Original negatives donated by soldiers, relatives or others. The Australian War Memorial retains most of these, and is fortunate that this mostly nitrate collection has shown minimal deterioration over the last eighty years. Caption books were also compiled for this series.

P: Prints and negatives lent or donated to the Australian War Memorial by soldiers or their relatives or others post-1983. The prefix is still in use.

H: Donated original prints. These cover all topics but about 50 per cent are portraits of deceased service personnel and were received in the 1920s and 1930s in response to the Roll of Honour circulars sent out to next of kin.

D: Australian official photographs taken in Britain c. 1916-1919.